Women in the Professions

Women in the Professions

Edited by

Laurily Keir Epstein
Washington University

Lexington Books
D.C. Heath and Company
Lexington, Massachusetts
Toronto   London

Library of Congress Cataloging in Publication Data

Main entry under title:

Women in the professions.

Papers from a conference held at Washington University, St. Louis, Apr. 1975; sponsored by Monticello College Foundation and Washington University.
1. Women—United States—Congresses. 2. Professions—United States—Congresses. 3. Women—Employment—United States—Congresses. I. Epstein, Laurily Keir. II. Monticello College Foundation. III. Washington University, St. Louis.
HQ1426.W64   331.4'0973   75-18051
ISBN 0-669-00130-9

International Standard Book Number: 0-669-00130-9

Library of Congress Catalog Card Number: 75-18051

This volume is dedicated to
the trustees and staff of the
Monticello College Foundation

Contents

List of Figures   ix

List of Tables   xi

Introduction   xv

Chapter 1   **Success Motivation and Social Structure: Comments on Women and Achievement**
Cynthia Fuchs Epstein   1

Chapter 2   **Women in Academia: Today is Different**
Juanita M. Kreps   15

Chapter 3   **Recent Trends in the Employment of American Women**
James A. Sweet   25

Chapter 4   **Female Status: A New Population Policy**
Virginia Gray   67

Chapter 5   **Black Women Officeholders: The Case of State Legislators**
Jewel Prestage   81

Chapter 6   **Women as Voters: Their Maturation as Political Persons in American Society**
John J. Stucker   97

Chapter 7   **Government Policy and the Legal Status of Women**
Roxanne Barton Conlin   115

Chapter 8   **Alternatives for Social Change: The**
                 Future Status of Women
                 Carolyn Shaw Bell   123

                 Index   137

                 About the Contributors   143

                 About the Editor   145

List of Figures

3-1   Age Patterns of Employment for Birth
        Cohorts of Women   27

3-2   Synthetic Life Cycle of Labor Force
        Participation Patterns: 1973   28

3-3   Labor Force Participation Rates of Married
        Women, Spouse Present, by Presence of
        Children: 1951-1972   40

3-4   Labor Force Participation Rates of Married
        Women, Spouse Present, by Age, with No
        Children Under 18 Present: 1951-1972   42

List of Tables

1	Median Earnings Year-Round Full-Time Workers, by Sex: 1955-1973	xvi
2	Median Wage or Salary Income of Year-Round Full-Time Workers in 1973, by Sex and Nonfarm Occupation Group	xvii
3	Proportion of College and University Degrees Earned by Women: 1900-1970	xviii
4	U.S. Women in State Legislatures, by State: 1973	xix
3-1	Recent Trends in U.S. Fertility	30
3-2	Duration Standardized Recent Fertility Rates	35
3-3	Percent of Women Single, by Age: 1972 and 1960	36
3-4	Number of Women, Age 18-24, in the United States: 1950-1973	38
3-5	Rates of Continuation in School, by Age and Sex: 1960 and 1970	39
3-6	Labor Force Participation Rates of Married Women, Husband Present, by Presence and Age of Children: March, 1960-1974	41
3-7	Changes in Labor Force Participation Rates for Women, by Education and Age: 1959 and 1973	46
3-8	Employment Rates of Nonfarm Mothers of Young Children, by Education of Mother: 1970	47

3-9   Occupation Distribution of Married Women:
             1960 and 1973   48

3-10   Proportion Female in Selected Occupations:
             1960 and 1970   50

3-11   Median Annual Income by Age   52

3-12   Percentage Change in Female Median Earnings,
             by Age and Education: 1959-1969   52

3-13   Wife's Earnings as a Component of Family
             Income, for Married Couples in Which
             Wife Had Earnings: March 1963 and
             March 1973   53

3-14   Earnings of Wife as Percent of Family
             Income for Husband-Wife Families in
             Which Both Husband and Wife Had Earnings,
             Race and Age of Husband: 1973   54

3-15   Distribution of Women with Work Experience,
             by Weeks Worked and Usual Hours Worked
             per Week: 1958-1971   55

3-16   Labor Force Participation Rates for White
             and Nonwhite Married Women, by Family
             Status: March 1973   56

3-17   Occupation Distribution of Employed Women,
             for Nonwhite Women, Age 14-34 and 35 and
             Over: 1960 and 1973   58

3-18   Selected Occupational Measure for Selected
             Age and Education Groups of Females,
             by Race: 1960-1970   59

3-19   Attitudes Toward Traditional Sex-Based
             Division of Labor, Employment Rights of
             Women, Work and Maternal Role, and
             Sex-Difference Stereotypes and
             Socialization, by Age   61

4-1	Comparison of Means for Suffrage and Nonsuffrage States	72
4-2	Regression Results for Birth Rate Equations in States: 1920s	73
5-1	Black Women Legislators, Total Black Legislators and Black Percentage of Population by State	86
5-2	Education of Legislators, and Fathers and Mothers of Legislators	87
5-3	Occupation/Profession of Legislators	87
5-4	Age Ranges of Legislators	88
5-5	Marital Status of Black Women Legislators	88
5-6	Number of Children in Families of Black Women Legislators	89
5-7	Political Experience of Black Women Legislators	89
5-8	Views of Personal Expertise and Special Competence by Black Women Legislators	90
5-9	Reelection Plans for Black Women State Legislators	90
5-10	Ambitions for Higher Office of Black Women Legislators	91
5-11	Views on Future of Women in Politics and Blacks in Politics	91
5-12	Views on Women's Liberation by Black Women Legislators	91
6-1	Dates When School Suffrage Grants to Women Were Made Effective by State Legislative Action or Change of State Constitution	99

6-2   Full and Presidential Suffrage Rights to Women Made Effective by Legislative Action or Constitutional Change at the State Level   101

6-3   Percentage Point Difference Scores on Four Electoral Indices, Differences Between Two Elections Before and Two Elections After Women Suffrage, National and Five Regions   104

6-4   Sex Differences in Voting in Presidential Elections: 1948-1972   107

6-5   Sex Differences in Voting in 1972 Presidential Election, National and Regional   107

6-6   Sex Differences in Presidential Voting by Age Group: 1964, 1968, and 1972   108

6-7   Sex Differences in Voting in 1972 Presidential Election by Age Grouping and Race   109

Introduction

This volume is the result of a two-day conference on the status of women in higher education and the professions held at Washington University in St. Louis in April, 1975. The conference was sponsored jointly by the Monticello College Foundation and Washington University as part of an important new program, the Mr. and Mrs. Spencer T. Olin Fellowship Program for Women, named for two leading benefactors of the Monticello College Foundation. This program began in the Fall of 1974; it provides four full years of fellowship support for outstanding women seeking a Ph.D. or a terminal degree in higher education and the professions at Washington University. Students are chosen on the basis of a nationwide competition and matriculate at Washington University in any one of the graduate or professional schools there.

In conjunction with the creation of the Olin Fellowship Program, it was deemed helpful to host a conference on the role of women in higher education and the professions in an attempt to provide an orderly examination of the very special problems women face today, and, in all likelihood, will face in the future, in playing an active role in their chosen fields. The conference was designed to bring together a group of scholars who had systematically analyzed various aspects of women's status in American society. Since women's status is a necessarily broad topic, this conference was structured in such a way that the central emphasis was drawn from the social sciences; that is, by the mid-1970s, there is a need for systematic investigation of the governmental policies of the last decade as well as a need to assess the known demographic trends of the society in which we live. Having passed beyond the threshold of consciousness raising, insightful analysis is more useful than mere rhetoric.

Enough data has been generated to demonstrate that women's status in the mid-1970s is still not comparable to that of men's position in society. Examples of the available data are found in the following tables: Table 1 lists median earnings for year-round full-time workers by sex for the years 1955-1973; Table 2 lists the median wage or salary income of year-round full-time workers in 1973 by sex; Table 3 lists the percentage of women receiving degrees in higher education from 1900-1970; and Table 4 lists the number and percent of women holding office in state legislatures in 1973.

Table 1 demonstrates that, despite the Equal Pay Act of 1963, Title VII of the 1964 Civil Rights Act, and Executive Order 11246 as amended in 1968, the average woman earned 56.6 percent of what the average man earned in 1973. This average is 7.3 percent lower than the comparable figure in 1955. Given the intent of the three laws mentioned above, this discrepancy is a bit startling.

Since the average woman works in different occupations than the average man, it is instructive to look at Table 2, presenting the mean wage or salary income by sex for nonfarm occupational groups. One finds that, in 1973,

Table 1

Median Earnings Year-Round Full-Time Workers, by Sex: 1955-1973 (Persons 14 Years of Age and Over)

| Year | Median Earnings | | Women's Median Earnings as Percent of Men's |
	Women	Men	
1973	$6,335	$11,186	56.6%
1972	5,903	10,202	57.9
1971	5,593	9,399	59.5
1970	5,323	8,966	59.4
1969	4,977	8,227	60.5
1968	4,457	7,664	58.2
1967	4,150	7,182	57.8
1966	3,973	6,848	58.0
1965	3,823	6,375	60.0
1964	3,690	6,195	59.6
1963	3,561	5,978	59.6
1962	3,446	5,794	59.5
1961	3,351	5,644	59.4
1960	3,293	5,417	60.8
1959	3,193	5,209	61.3
1958	3,102	4,927	63.0
1957	3,008	4,713	63.8
1956	2,827	4,466	63.3
1955	2,719	4,252	63.9

Note: For 1967-1973 data include wage and salary income and earnings from self-employment; for 1955-1966, data include wage and salary income only.

Source: Women's Bureau of the U.S. Department of Labor from data published by the Bureau of the Census, U.S. Department of Commerce, March 1975.

professional women earned 65.2 percent of what professional men earned. In 1956, the comparable figure was 62.4 percent. For sales workers, women earned 38.8 percent of what men earned in 1973; in 1956, the figure was 41.8 percent. The figures for other broad occupational categories vary within these ranges. None of the figures are particularly encouraging in terms of what one would expect for genuine wage equalization between the sexes.

Table 3 presents data for women in higher education during this century. Here it is instructive to note that, in 1970, the proportion of women receiving doctorates was below the proportions in 1920 and 1930. Data on women in higher education during the 1970s indicate that women are increasing their number in higher education but, at the upper levels, there remain large differences.

Table 2

Median Wage or Salary Income of Year-Round Full-Time Workers in 1973, by Sex and Nonfarm Occupation Group (Persons 14 Years of Age and Over)

Major Occupation Group	Median Wage or Salary Income		Women's Median Wage or Salary Income as Percent of Men's
	Women	Men	
Professional, technical workers	$9,095	$13,945	65.2
Managers, administrators (except farm)	7,998	14,737	54.3
Sales workers	4,674	12,031	38.8
Clerical workers	6,458	10,619	60.8
Craft and kindred workers	6,315	11,308	55.8
Operatives (including transport)	5,420	9,481	57.2
Service workers (except private household)	4,745	8,112	58.5
Private household workers	2,243	[a]	—
Nonfarm laborers	5,286	8,037	65.8

[a]Fewer than 75,000 men.

Source: Women's Bureau of the U.S. Department of Labor from data published by the Bureau of the Census, U.S. Department of Commerce, March 1975.

Finally, Table 4 presents information on women in the state legislatures in 1973. The November 1974 elections saw more women elected but not in sufficient numbers to alter these data significantly.

The data presented above are interesting and instructive but do not speak for themselves. They are meant to serve as a starting point for this volume's analysis. The eight chapters of the book present a variety of viewpoints and types of analysis of women's status in the mid-1970s.

In Chapter 1, Cynthia Fuchs Epstein deals with a set of long-held assumptions that women either do not want to succeed or are unable to do so. In particular, she examines and refutes a set of alleged scientific ideas that help perpetuate the expectation that women and success are incompatible. In Chapter 2, Juanita Kreps compares the position of women in academia in today's market with that of several decades ago. Her predictions for the future of academic women are based on what the economy and known demographic facts will do to the hiring and placement of both sexes. Chapter 3, written by James Sweet, presents an extraordinarily comprehensive overview of the observed changes in women's role in the labor force since the end of World War II.

After reviewing briefly what she calls "the social context of reproductive

Table 3
Proportion of College and University Degrees Earned by Women: 1900-1970

Year	Bachelor's	Master's	Ph.D.'s
1900	19.7	19.1	6.0
1910	22.7	26.4	9.9
1920	34.2	30.2	15.1
1930	39.9	40.4	15.4
1940	41.6	38.3	13.0
1950	23.9	29.2	9.7
1960	35.3	35.1	10.5
1970	41.5	39.7	13.3

Source: U.S. Bureau of the Census, "Historical Statistics of the United States" (Washington, D.C.: U.S. Government Printing Office, 1961).

decisions," Virginia Gray, author of Chapter 4, assesses the effects of suffrage on birth rates. The results of her analysis demonstrate that governmental policies favoring women's equality can have a measurable impact on fertility rates. Her findings lead her to stress the need for a new population policy, allowing women a genuine set of alternatives between rigid pronatalism and antinatalism.

Chapters 5 and 6 deal with women and politics. Chapter 5, written by Jewel Prestage, presents original interview data from black women state legislators. The author interprets the data within the larger theoretical framework of American political participation and socialization processes. Her findings demonstrate that there are sharp differences between black women and black men, and between black and white women. John Stucker, author of Chapter 6, reviews evidence of both the historical and contemporary political differences between the sexes in terms of voting behavior and other forms of participatory activity. He concludes with several pertinent observations: men and women must equalize their economic roles before their political roles are equalized; and there remain strong differences in the activities and perceptions between black and white women.

Chapter 7's author, Roxanne Barton Conlin, presents a brief but concise review of the federal legislation designed to broaden women's rights beginning with the Equal Pay Act of 1963. She concludes that, despite the recent flurry of legislation to ameliorate sex-based discrimination, the legal battle for equality is far from completion.

The concluding chapter, written by Carolyn Shaw Bell, presents a unique and imaginative set of proposals to hasten the dawn of genuine sex-based equality. Her proposals go beyond "soft programs"; in lieu of these, she recognizes the social importance of restructuring of economic policies.

In closing, it should be noted that this volume is not intended to be a final statement on women's status. It is intended to furnish the reader with a

Table 4
U.S. Women in State Legislatures, by State: 1973

State	Proportion	Number
Alabama	.007	1/141
Alaska	.100	6/60
Arizona	.133	12/90
Arkansas	.037	5/135
California	.025	3/120
Colorado	.090	9/100
Connecticut	.107	20/187
Delaware	.080	5/62
Florida	.043	7/160
Georgia	.025	6/236
Hawaii	.039	3/76
Idaho	.057	6/105
Illinois	.046	11/236
Indiana	.060	9/150
Iowa	.066	10/150
Kansas	.042	7/165
Kentucky	.043	6/138
Louisiana	.020	2/144
Maine	.097	18/184
Maryland	.064	12/185
Massachusetts	.039	11/280
Michigan	.054	8/148
Minnesota	.029	6/201
Mississippi	.040	7/174
Missouri	.065	13/197
Montana	.053	8/150
Nebraska	.013	2/149
Nevada	.083	5/60
New Hampshire	.209	89/424
New Jersey	.062	8/129
New Mexico	.017	2/112
New York	.028	6/210
North Carolina	.058	10/170
North Dakota	.071	11/153
Ohio	.052	8/153
Oklahoma	.013	2/149
Oregon	.137	11/180
Pennsylvania	.027	7/253
Rhode Island	.040	6/150

Table 4 (cont.)

State	Proportion	Number
South Carolina	.047	8/170
South Dakota	.057	6/105
Tennessee	.030	4/132
Texas	.044	8/181
Utah	.086	9/104
Vermont	.122	22/180
Virginia	.042	6/140
Washington	.074	11/147
West Virginia	.067	9/134
Wisconsin	.045	6/133
Wyoming	.065	6/92

Source: Adapted from *Women's Rights Almanac 1974*, Nancy Gager, ed., Bethesda, Maryland: Stanton, 1974.

comprehensive background on many of the salient issues confronting women in the years ahead.

Special thanks are extended to the Monticello College Foundation and to Lattie F. Coor, University Vice Chancellor, and Ralph E. Morrow, Dean of the Graduate School of Arts and Sciences, Washington University (St. Louis). It was their concern for women in the professions that led to the possibility of this volume.

L.K.E.

Women in the Professions

1

Success Motivation and Social Structure: Comments on Women and Achievement

Cynthia Fuchs Epstein

Getting more and becoming more have been core values in American society from the days of the Founding Fathers. The extent to which they are values lodged in other societies varies a great deal, but this does not wholly eradicate the possibility that some set of drives toward improvement are universal for all humans and are linked to capacities and dispositions to walk; talk; control one's bodily functions; satisfy one's needs; and, generally, to learn.

Of course, as with anything that seems basic and universal for the human species, culture interacts with individual needs and capacities so as to structure, direct, and often inhibit them altogether.

So it has been generally for the *goals* of humans, whether they have been goals such as the acquisition of food or shelter—directed toward survival—or abstract and symbolic goals such as the attainment of prestige and honor, good taste, or love.

The culture of any society normally dictates *how* any goal may be achieved, such as by allocation or conquest; the *form* a goal should take, for example, whether steak or grasshoppers are to be defined as a great meal; and *who* may seek the goal—whether, for example, a man or a woman may command the army to victory. (You will recall Joan of Arc had no trouble in this regard.)

All of these considerations are important in analyzing how women have attempted to seek the goal of success and the extent to which they have been not only prevented from achieving success, but taught to feel it wrong that they should do so.

Of course, the general success goals differ from society to society. In some, living the good life means getting enough money to be able to sit around in silken robes and read poetry; in American society, success has meant making money, but not necessarily lounging about. Further, making money has been linked to acquiring power, the acquisition of material comforts, and the right to acquire still more money! It also means the power to influence others and to be free from influence by others.

There is some question as to whether or not definitions regarding what it means to be successful differ between men and women. Although men and women learn that one or the other sex is deemed "appropriate" to work for this or that set of life's delights, they both seem to prize the same ones. By this I mean to emphasize that there is no male value system different from a female value system.

1

Furthermore, value goals for the whole society seem to emanate from the upper stratum. People or rank and prestige set the style; most typically people in the lesser positions tend to believe the goals of the powerful are the important ones, although they know they will be in no position to acquire them themselves. Because men are the rulers in most societies, the valued goals in these societies are those of the men in power. Thus, where combat is prized by the males in power, women tend to fall in love with knights and think that war is a wonderful activity. Where men prize stocks and bonds, women tend to rate the acquisition of these in the same way. (They learn to want to acquire the men who will acquire the stocks and bonds.)

There are more than a few unstated assumptions in these comments. They include one which indicates that, most typically, women have not been supposed to be the ones to acquire valued things independently. They have been, as Jean Lipman-Blumen has pointed out, vicarious achievers.[1] Of course, there has been change in this set of attitudes, but not enough to make the observation no longer current.

In alluding to the Founding Fathers of our nation when describing success values in American society, it may be noted I omitted the women who were around at the same time—not because there were no mothers involved in the founding, but because the United States of America were under the control and jurisdiction of the fathers. It was they who assigned women their jobs and place in American society and they who continue to make the decisions.

What follows will present some lines of reasoning and argument regarding women's capacity to share with men the valued things in American life and their opportunity to rise in the mobility structure, which is the American way of success.

First is to debate the idea that women have no particular will, desire, or ambition for success. Rather, there is an entrenched theoretical framework underpinning that set of assumptions. That is, the set of ideas itself serves as a mechanism to keep women in their place and out of the competition for the good things in life and to keep them from achieving power over these assumptions. Furthermore, the structure of our society works hand in glove with the structure of our thinking to create the most minimal access for women.

Today, women are at the height of their consciousness regarding their exclusion from the channels to top opportunities. It is true that there were great feminists in days past who saw through the veils of myths and attitudes about women, but only today are there masses of women geared to what is going on.

There is no longer any question that there has been and still is exclusion. Although much of my work has focussed on isolating and identifying the less visible processes, I believe that it is ever more important today because there is a good chance they will become even more subtle and invisible than before. I am, for example, currently interested in showing the consequences of seemingly innocent or seemingly "scientific" ideas, and will show how we tend to accept frameworks that seem to be scientific and use them against ourselves and those we mean to help.

Some time ago, Robert Merton identified the process he called "unanticipated consequences of purposive social action."[2] As part of this process, he showed that often well-intentioned plans have negative or destructive outcomes. One example of this is the creation of low-income housing, still going on and still well intentioned, which does serve one intended purpose of providing inexpensive housing for those people who cannot afford better shelter for themselves. However, these projects also create ghettos with separate and unequal schooling for the children, anomic societies lacking in community organization, and areas of high crime.

Unanticipated consequences also flow from the work of other well-intentioned people. Teachers, college administrators, guidance counselors, placement officers, and personnel agents, systematically and over the years, have pressed blacks and women into educational programs that geared them for "practical" positions—those in which they could either get jobs and thus not face discriminatory practices, or those that were believed coordinated with their capacities or role obligations: low-level technical training for blacks, social work and teacher-training for girls.

What was the consequence? When pressures on economic gatekeepers let down some of the most blatant barriers, there were insufficient pools of eligible recruits with formal training for other jobs—higher level jobs. Blacks and women not only had been trained to do other things, they also had been convinced they were incapable of trying the new opportunities because there were innate incapacities that arose from their sex or racial status. They would not be *interested* in the areas from which they were formerly excluded—women and blacks didn't like business, science, and engineering.

Even worse than knowing they wouldn't like a particular kind of work was the knowledge that certain work was unsuitable. Blacks were instructed to abhor the world of the white and were not supposed to join his world, his culture, or his establishments. Women knew it was unladylike to do the masculine work of science or engineering and, worse still, to issue commands, particularly to men. Furthermore, women knew that they were not supposed to be interested in raises and promotions, they weren't supposed to like power, and they weren't supposed to be comfortable in making their own decisions.

How did they know these things? Men told them; other women told them. Fathers, mothers, husbands, and maiden aunts told them. Furthermore, their teachers, guidance counselors, and girl friends told them. But even more insidious—they read it was so in books of psychology, measurement, and testing.

Women measured low in interest for the things they were not supposed to be able to do or weren't supposed to like. The measurement proved it all. As a result they weren't admitted to programs that used the tests as an indicator of motivation and capacity—from activities such as college to management training programs. A girl who bypassed all this knew she was a deviant—pathological. She often had to go to the psychiatrist who certainly told her that she had adjustment problems; that her goals were not reality oriented; that she had fantasies growing out of neurotic needs; and that her ambitions or interests were a cover-up for an unresolved Oedipus complex. At best she had penis envy; at worst she wanted to kill her father.

The scientific views that were a majority in psychoanalysis followed in the traditions of Aristotle, Nietzsche, and the Old and New Testaments. Somehow, competing views—some of Plato, of John Stuart Mill, and later, Karen Horney—didn't catch the popular imagination.

This is not because they were less philosophically logical or scientifically sound, but because the gatekeepers—males in power—preferred one kind of explanation to another. That is, men in power—whether they be kings, legislators, captains of industry, or professors of scientific institutions—always prefer religions or philosophies that justify their position and argue that the rulers are by nature, and not nurture, more gifted, more beautiful, more suitable, more able, or more smiled upon by the deity.

We might have expected to hear from those at the top that they were there by virtue of competence, and that opening the gates would mean a lessening in caliber of the post or position, resulting in the entire system experiencing deficiency. Richard A. Lester recently reported to the Carnegie Commission that Affirmative Action programs in the universities meant a lessening of quality, arguing that blacks and women don't have the same training or experience as the white male professors.[3] He justified his argument by saying that the fact that there were no women or black full professors in universities indicated that they were of poorer quality, less creative, and less productive.

Furthermore, a number of sociologists, today, are arguing and attempting to prove that science is universalistic and that all that matters to top administrators is who produces the great papers and great ideas. They would accept women if they produced anything of equal merit. They point out that women probably could produce these ideas if they had *earlier* socialization and training, but it has typically been *too late* by the time the free and open system of evaluation in science takes over.

In another vein, but in associated argument, Matina Horner, now President of Radcliffe College, reported a study in *Psychology Today* which catapulted her into fame.[4] It showed that women students of excellent ability had a psychological fear of success which presumably hindered them from striving for the achievement of their highest potential. Her views were embraced by educators of antifeminist and feminist positions alike.

The "fear of success" idea suggested that the *reason* women had not become great poets, professors, or jurists, was because they feared being recognized as achievers. The feminists liked this idea because it didn't assert that women weren't able to write or paint or think, but that the fear of doing too well at any of these activities prevented them from working at them to full capacity.

Antifeminists did not herald these findings as vociferously, but they too accepted the views that, for them, served the purpose of corroborating the ideas *they* had held all along: that women weren't made of the same stuff as men—they weren't hard-driving or highly motivated and they feared what men dared!

Here was "science" being used again to serve essentially opposite value positions, and worse, being misinterpreted.

The findings tapped some meaningful responses. Although typical of all women, University of Michigan girls certainly constitute a corps of educated, able women. If *they* didn't have motivation and drive to do well, what could one expect of the merely competent and average?

My female friends and colleagues told each other that now they knew why they had had a rough time rising in the system. It wasn't anybody else's fault—it was their *own* fear of success that put limits on their careers.

Once again, one could see how insidious were the consequences of this way of thinking. If one blames early socialization, he also accepts the futility of trying to do something about the present situation.

This also serves the purpose of diverting blame from those who are responsible for discrimination and prejudice. After all, if women don't want to become supervisors, leaders, scientists, or administrators of programs, then employers can't be faulted for denying them jobs.

Permit me, for a moment, to press this observation to logical extremes. The consequences of Matina Horner's study—the way in which it was interpreted and the way in which it was received—link to what we know about the social psychology of abuse. We have recently found, for example, that those who torment or torture others end up blaming the victim; and that sometimes, the victim ends up blaming himself.

From the mother who spanks her child screaming, "You asked for this!" to the American soldier in Vietnam who was persuaded that the Vietcong soldiers were less-than-human and were asking for punishment—this mechanism of blaming the victim seems lodged in human psychology and also acts as a mechanism for leaders or groups and societies to assert their own superiority and exoneration from responsibility for their fellow human beings.

Where science is used to "prove" inferiority, it is most insidious because people are less suspicious of scientists than they are of political leaders.

Certainly women have suffered seriously from the claims of science regarding their capacity and interests. For women there are not just a few Jensens or Hernnsteins who provide proof of women's inability to deal with such things as abstract reasoning or spatial relations, but many. The challenges of these assertions are only beginning to emerge.

To return to the Horner study, her evidence was the performance of women college students who had been subjects in her research on achievement motivation. Her tests measured a state of mind—that of uneasiness. She did not measure whether the fears found to be characteristic of the women college students actually did inhibit their striving in real life. The women she tested came out higher in anxiety than the men she tested when responding to verbal leads regarding success cues. They composed stories to complete this lead: "After first term finals, Anne finds herself at the top of her medical school class." The completed stories scored high in "fear of success imagery."[5] But was it fear of success that actually created anxiety? Horner does suggest that women fear not the prize of honor or money or prestige. What they fear is the punishment that goes along with those rewards—punishment that men don't get. No man who gets a promotion or more money or an award is accused of being not-a-man they way a woman is accused of being not-a-woman for the same achievements. The woman is accused of being emmasculating; hard; aggressive; fearsome; and, perhaps, loathesome. With occupational success the man is seen as achieving the height of his manhood. Friends and family applaud him while the woman who achieves these honors receives mixed reviews and suspicions. Her parents wonder whether her achievements have been accomplished at the expense of her children's mental health. Her employers wonder how the men in the work team will receive the news.

The woman moving towards success knows she will not be unequivocally blessed and she fears those ambivalent reactions. She fears the *punishment* attached to the reward, not the reward! However, I doubt whether women actually strive to *avoid* success because of their fears of punishment. It seems to me that Horner's conclusion that there is present in many women "a stable, enduring personality characteristic"—a "motive to avoid success."[6]

It is further suggested that if we were to make a study of women who achieve success occupationally and do not suffer those punishing reactions from salient others in their life, it would show no more anxiety present than in men in the same situation. We must remind ourselves that all people fear added responsibilities or a change in the structure of their lives. They fear the tests that will prove or disprove their abilities. For those who have passed from a transitional status and have proven their competence, not only do their anxiety levels drop, but they feel better than before. How terrible to go through life always wondering if you have the stuff—how much more wonderful to have passed the exams, done well at the interview, gotten the degree! In fact, a recent replication of the Horner study showed that in Horner's terms, fear of success imagery was present in 73 percent of the stories from a comparable group of college students at the University of Buffalo. There was no difference by sex.[7]

This study seriously challenged the methodology of the Horner study and also remarked on the curiosity that a limited study should produce such notice in the professional community.

Horner's work suggests that the fears women have go back to their early socialization. We hear a great deal about early socialization and its importance today. In reaction we are becoming more acute to the sexist terminology in books and in the media.

However, it may be that too much weight has been placed on this particular problem. Focussing too much on early socialization has negative consequences—once we believe all the damage was done early, we write off an entire generation as essentially incapable of being changed. Again, gatekeepers in business and the professions can pass the buck to the educators who made girls study home economics while the boys trained in science. "It's not our fault," they assert, "that women aren't trained to become managers. They were socialized to be passive, docile, and retiring." Now, no doubt some of this is true, but it is apparent that the early socialization model of child development has certain racist and particularly sexist ramifications.

There is an alternative to the early socialization model, underrepresented in current thought—both popular and scientific. It is a model of ongoing development—the framework that asserts that personality is not set early and is therefore unchangeable. However, it is capable of change through a person's lifetime, and quite radical change at that.

The reason it appears that personality is set early is because people are tracked in channels where they are not apt to receive different messages later in life than they had earlier; that once having been labelled as being of a particular personality type and having a particular capacity, structure conspires to reinforce that view. Thus a child who is labelled bright in science will be so defined through life by his intimates unless reality considerations are so discrepant with that label as to force change. It is worse for the child who is labelled stupid, emotional, or erratic. He or she is subtly reinforced in his behaviors and develops an unchallenged self-image and set of aspirations consonant with that label.

My initial cues regarding this model came when, after the women's movement had been sufficiently developed so as to make career opportunities available to many women, I could see distinct changes in the personalities of women. Those who had severe self-doubts regarding their own competence found that when they were given additional responsibility they could handle it well, although they were scared to begin with. Women who were afraid of taking jobs normally reserved for men found they could not only learn things they thought they couldn't (like the economics of magazine production), but found they liked the new activity. They also liked the power and they liked the success. Nothing, it seems, succeeds like success.

Of course women with no science training did not become nuclear physicists overnight. However, there are many jobs in which most learning occurs on the job and the only prerequisite is sufficient intelligence. What is also needed is a lot of support and confidence from those who assign the job and from others in the environment.

Who learns, for example, to be a congressman or woman before being elected? At best, the person demonstrates some competence with public issues. Plenty of good legislators never had any experience. They learn on the job, and they change on the job. Some fail, of course, but it is hard to predict who will fail—the definition of success and failure depends upon your own view of what ought to be done. Presidents Ford, Johnson, Kennedy, or Lincoln didn't have experience being president of anything, yet all were deemed able to assume the office of the president.

There is a difference between working in an environment where everyone is geared to expecting your success and one in which everyone is geared to your failure. Women have most typically faced situations where it was assumed they would fail in supervising male-dominated assignments. They were not given the treatment a boss gives to a protege—putting an arm across the shoulders of "his boy" and introducing him as being the most likely to succeed. They have typically been told they couldn't or wouldn't make it—not just in primary school, but in high school, through college entrance, to the job. Women have been told they would fail in science programs, in law programs, and in business administration. They have been diverted from channels that would put them in contact with those who were in a position to further their careers or in which they would learn important inside ideas regarding what it takes to make it in the system.

Even today women are told they need special programs for women, to make up for the deficiencies of the past. Some administrators of the few remaining women's colleges believe women need to be specially protected; that they don't do as well in learning environments with men. In a sense it is believed they can garner strength in the protected environment of the women's college which can be put to use later. I doubt this. The real world is composed of men and women. Both need to learn to relate to the other. Women and men need to learn to reach each other—to operate in each other's worlds.

There is a logical "fit" to the view of a *continuing* model of socialization and the capacity for significant change, and to policy decisions regarding women and the routes to mobility. With good planning and restructuring of environments which are, at the moment, punishing, women can do better and get farther than has been believed possible. They can do this without waiting for the future generations to grow up to be educated free of sexist school books and exposure to models of mindless mothers on the television.

Of course, it is not enough to assert this can be done; or use only anecdotal materials. While scientific evidence for this position is sparse, there are a number of studies from various disciplines that are supportive of the thesis of personality development and change.

First, there are some startling findings in animal studies. In an article by Neal Miller the work of Fuller is reported.[8] Fuller and his associates reared puppies in isolation from the ages of three to twelve weeks. Early isolation experience is known to produce long-lasting deficits in the social and manipulative responses of animals and children. We have believed that there is a sensitive period in the learning of the types of behavior in which the deprived dogs were deficient, and that the dog loses his capacity for the type of learning required after the sensitive period is over. However, Fuller found that if puppies reared in isolation were given a tranquilizer, chlorpromazine, during their first test session, they became relaxed and this enabled them to learn at a later stage of development than seemed possible before. These observations indicated that gradual learning at an "appropriate" stage was important, but that the puppies could learn quickly and *later* in test conditions using the drug. Why did puppies not put on the drug fail to learn? Fuller found that it was not the deprivation per se that caused lasting damage but the sudden emergence from isolation that elicited traumatic fears which were learned and interfered with the performance and/or rapid learning of behavior of which the animal was perfectly capable. The trauma was avoided by the temporary use of tranquilizers at this crucial juncture.

The notion of "critical periods" was similarly reviewed by Hinde[9] and Moltz[10] by using birds. Similar use of tranquilizers made it possible for birds to learn beyond the period in which it was believed they had to be exposed to learning. What we find from these studies is not that animals or people lose their capacity to learn if they don't learn early, but that they develop fears regarding *new* learning which may inhibit them. Removing the fear in the animal case by use of tranquilizers, or, as suggested in the case of women—by substituting rewards for punishments, may in fact increase the capacity for acquisition of new skills and attitudes towards those skills.

Work by Seymour Epstein and Walter Fenz examined the avoidance activity characteristic of people when they approach goals that are difficult or fearsome.[11] They studied changes in anxiety levels of novice parachutists from the University of Massachusetts Sport Parachuting Club. The finding of this study which most interests me is one that showed that ancillary benefits came from the actual successful first jump. This mastery over a fearsome event apparently reduced conflict and fear in other areas. The father of one parachutist reported that his son, a chronic stutterer, experienced an alleviation of symptoms on the afternoon following his first jump. Another subject noted his increased frustration tolerance following a parachute jump. He noted that although he experienced a terrible feeling of loss of face and ego when turned down by a girl, after the parachute jump he could slough off the rejection.[12] Success makes for more success, more coping, more capacity to learn.

Perhaps the strongest cases for proving the possibility of change after early childhood and because of situational placement, have been done by Jerome Kagan and Melvin Kohn and their associates at the Institute of Nutrition of Central America and Panama, Guatemala.[13] Kagan and Klein in their cross-national study of early development, report that from birth to three years of age Guatemalan Indians of the rural northwest were passive, quiet, and timid, but eleven-year-olds were active, gay, and intellectually competent.

They offer the suggestion that implies absence of a predictive relationship between level of cognitive development at twelve-eighteen months of age and quality of intellectual functioning at eleven years.

Moreover, Kagan and Klein say, these observations suggest that it is misleading to talk about continuity of any psychological characteristic, be it cognitive, motivational, or behavioral, without specifying simultaneously the context of development.

In the Indian village studied, by eight years of age some of the passive children became dominant over others because the structure of the peer group required that the role be filled.

Research by Melvin Kohn and Carmi Schooler shows that people's self-esteem is related to the complexity of their job and that it is not true that those with a prior orientation toward self-direction will be led to jobs that demand autonomy.[14] More generally, Kohn and Schooler demonstrate that the correlation between psychological functioning and job conditions is large enough to indicate causality from that direction. The qualities demonstrated were being more intellectually flexible, being more intellectually demanding, having more personally responsible moral standards, being more receptive to change, being less anxious, having greater self-esteem, and being more self-directed in their values.

We may also note that the quality of intellectual flexibility has as its most particular determinants, education and *substantive complexity* of the work. The impact greatly surpassed age, race, natural background, and region of the country in which the person was raised.[15]

Of course this experimental evidence is nothing compared with large amounts of historical data we have prior to the industrial revolution that indicated that any number of populations of women showed remarkable competence in the handling of business and financial affairs growing out of family enterprises they inherited or they ran in the absence of spouses due to war or adventure. Ann Oakely's new book on housewives shows how, when women were given the opportunity, they could, without apprenticeships or formal training, become printers, brewers, textile workers, innkeepers, ironmongers, managers of farms, and so on.[16] Oakely reports on sixteenth and seventeenth century England. We also have similar evidence in colonial America. The common variable, of course, was opportunity. Women who were given opportunities to learn, did so. They did so without early training and without the early psychological preparation that these activities were to become their careers.

Elsewhere it is shown that almost all women legislators in the United States became so because of the death of a husband and with only the casual learning they acquired at being close to the action and the later support of an interested constituency.

The staggering increases of women in medical and law schools and, lately, in graduate schools of business administration, is further evidence that early socialization can be overcome. Young women of the early 1970s and today have no different nursing, doll-playing, or father seduction than did their sisters of the

1960s. They chose male occupational training as soon as it became available and it seemed to promise rewarding possibilities.

We might consider what this thesis means in terms of social policy devoted to increasing the chance for the mobility of women. In schools, at all levels from primary grades to college, we believe freedom to choose courses and programs of learning gives women no freedom whatsoever. All it does is reinforce them in the old ruts and stereotypes the culture has already imposed on them.

Women probably ought to be encouraged and *required* to study a wide range of subjects, including the sciences, economics, and law. Only then can they be exposed to what these fields are and acquire competence in them which will be encouraging to their future activity in any of these areas.

Furthermore, women who show any interest in a sphere in which they are not sufficiently prepared by the rule book, ought to be encouraged to go into the field anyway. If interested, they can make up their deficiencies. Women ought *not* be in special programs geared to women. Ultimately, these are watered down programs. Instead, women ought to have good counseling—people they can go to who will give them confidence and sympathy and hard, good advice.

Women should be assigned to sponsoring professors who will be responsible for their advancement and have a vested interest in their survival. Perhaps professors ought to be denied grants unless they are training women students as well as men. We should have fewer requirements for entrance to programs of learning whether in colleges or in career situations. Employers ought to assign one experienced person to help guide a new woman employee—not throw her in the arena and see if she swims. Let's motivate the gatekeepers to bring women in.

We need to continue to explore the sexist nature of our scientific theories and research programs which may have the consequence of reinforcing stereotyped views that otherwise seem progressive and open.

I realize that some of these suggestions would be hard to implement. They fly in the face of rules and bylaws. They face entrenched stereotypes regarding people's capacities and futures.

The attitudes that create opportunity have a similarity with regard to people or to science. We ought to ask, "Why not?" rather than "why?"—in determining capacities. We need to be careful in locating what is real and what is illusion. In science, seeing what is causing incentive and motivation; and in the occupations, indicating to women what is real opportunity and what is a mere response to current legislative pressure.

For example, too many women today with so-called managerial and administrative jobs are not really on the track to top jobs. As Special Assistant to the President in charge of affirmative action, or as head of a Women's Studies Program, they are still in ancillary roles or in women's ghettos.

Upward mobility for women should be in the mainstream of the hierarchy, not on parallel and separate courses. We must not let this happen in education, the occupations, or in science. We would be foolish not to expect many subtle and diversionary moves intended to keep women separate from those who must now compete with the talent women have always had and now plan and expect to use.

Notes

1. Jean Lipman-Blumen, "The Vicarious Achievement Ethic and Nontraditional Roles for Women," unpublished paper, 1973.

2. Robert K. Merton, *Social Theory and Social Structure* (Riverside, N.J.: Free Press, 1957).

3. Richard A. Lester, *Antibias Regulation of Universities,* A Report prepared for the Carnegie Commission on Higher Education (New York: McGraw-Hill, 1974).

4. Matina Horner, "Fail: Bright Women," *Psychology Today* 3, no. 36 (November, 1969), pp. 62 ff.

5. Matina Horner, "Sex Differences in Achievement Motivation and Performance in Competitive and Non-Competitive Situations" (Ph.D. dissertation, University of Michigan, 1968), p. 105.

6. Matina Horner, "Femininity and Successful Achievement: A Basic Inconsistency," in Judith Bardwick, et al., eds., *Feminine Personality and Conflict* (Belmont, California: Brooks/Cole, 1970), p. 47.

7. Adeline Levine and Janice Crumrine, "Women and the Fear of Success: A Problem in Replication," *American Journal of Sociology* 80, no. 4 (January, 1975), pp. 964-974.

8. Neal E. Miller, "Some Implications of Modern Behavior Theory for Personality Change and Psychotherapy," in Gardner Lindzey and Calvin S. Hall eds., *Theories of Personality: Primary Sources and Research* (New York: Wiley, 1965), pp. 413-429.

9. R.A. Hinde, "The Modifiability of Instinctive Behavior," *The Advancement of Science* 12 (1955), pp. 19-24.

10. H. Moltz, "Inprinting: Empirical Basis and Theoretical Significance," *Psychological Bulletin* 57 (1960), pp. 291-314.

11. Seymour Epstein and Walter D. Fenz, "Theory and Experiment on the Measurement of Approach-Avoidance Conflict," in Gardner Lindzey and Calvin S. Hall, eds., op. cit., pp. 444-459.

12. Ibid., p. 457.

13. Jerome Kagan and Robert E. Klein, "Cross-Cultural Perspectives on Early Development," *American Psychologist* 28, no. 3 (November, 1973), pp. 947-961.

14. Melvin Kohn and Carmi Schooler, "Occupational Experience and Psychological Functioning: An Assessment of Reciprocal Effects," *American Sociological Review* 38 (February, 1973), pp. 97-118.

15. Ibid., p. 114.

16. Ann Oakley, *The Sociology of Housework* (London: Marton Robertson, 1974), p. 19.

2

Women in Academia: Today is Different

Juanita M. Kreps

The story of women in the academy has been told many times. With candor and good humour and occasionally with a touch of bitterness, women have related the rewards and frustrations inherent in this essentially "monastic" profession[1] which, notwithstanding its shortcomings, continues to hold great appeal for persons of both sexes. Recent accounts are strikingly different, however, from those that appeared in earlier times. It is not important to mourn yesterday, but it is important to note that today is different.

Today and Yesterday

When Jessie Bernard wrote her excellent analysis of *Academic Women* more than a decade ago, she reflected on the record of the past and concluded that

> ... academic women constitute a different population, statistically speaking, from academic men. In the world of academic women, career patterns develop along different lines. Women tend to serve in institutions which emphasize different functions, and they themselves are attracted to different kinds of functions. Further, they tend to be in areas which are not in strategic positions in the academic market place and which are not as productive as the areas that attract men.[2]

The record has clearly documented these sex differences in the recent past. The woman who took her doctoral degree in the era of the Second World War was likely to devote a substantial portion of her time to hearth and home, and sometimes apologize for having a career at all. In the 1950s, too, the woman scholar was both rare and subdued. Not until the sixties did a large proportion of women evidence strong career drives and greatly increased interest in the wide range of jobs that higher education offers. In that decade alone women's proportion of all Ph.D.'s increased by nearly one-third.

To young women in college today, career is a much more dominant theme. Home responsibilities and child care are taken seriously, but they are not all-consuming. Rather than fitting her career into those hours of the day left free of family obligations, the younger academic woman expects to be able to manage the household with a minimum of time, leaving her major energies for

15

research and teaching. Not only does she look forward to a continuous career; she also expects her family to cooperate fully with this aspiration.

The contrast between the woman college graduate of the 1940s who was going to marry and have six children, and the graduate of the 1970s who talks more of graduate or professional school, should tell us something of the future academic marketplace. It is not an altogether reliable predictor, of course. Just as earlier, we found ourselves fleeing back to jobs in the grimy, glamorous cities, (There was simply too much fresh air and floor wax out there in suburbia.) so, too, women graduates of the seventies may choose to redefine their priorities. We did not do precisely what we planned to do, and there is no reason to expect our daughters to do so.

However, there is at least one critical difference. That difference lies not just in women's expectations of themselves, significant as that factor is—it emerges also from society's expectation of women. In particular, society has decreed that women have equal job opportunities; that when qualified and hired, they receive equal pay; that their sex does not disqualify them from any academic post; and in brief, that when their performance in the workplace matches that of men, their rewards shall be equivalent.

These are bold new declarations. We have not yet had time to assess their impact on the aspirations and performance of the new generation of academic women. Nor has there been time to see whether or not the declarations will hold firm under the pressures now impinging on the institution, its hiring and promotion decisions. In addressing the question of today's professional woman, one must ask what kind of economy she will enter; what kind of institution she will serve; and ultimately, of course, what kind of woman she is. Let us take these in turn. What kind of economy are we facing? Is there any room for growth?

The Economy

For academic women, the timing is curious. Just when the numbers of women Ph.D.'s have begun to grow rapidly, the market for their talents (and those of male scholars) has begun to shrink. The academic job market is not likely to get better, moreover, in the near future. During the remainder of this century the numbers of college age youth will be declining, and although it would be possible to raise the proportion of youth and other age groups enrolled in post-secondary study, there does not seem to be strong sentiment for the public spending that such an increase would require. As a result of the downturn in enrollments, colleges and universities will not just cease hiring, they will also be letting people go. In faculty and staff cuts, seniority and tenure are likely to offer much more protection to men who have had continuous work histories, than to newly hired or part-time women.

When the job market is expanding, employers are prompted to reach further down the labor queue, hiring workers in the order of their attractiveness.[3] Which potential employee is attractive depends on the mind-set of the employer and the characteristics of the persons waiting to be hired. The sex of the applicant is an important characteristic, so important for some jobs and to some employers that only one sex is acceptable. Members of the other sex are then so far down the line that they have little chance of being employed in that job. In effect, they constitute a different queue altogether.

The great advantage of a tight labor market is the forced erosion of preconceptions and the acceptance of formerly unacceptable persons, who thenceforth can be considered on the basis of individual competence. For women, major breakthroughs have occurred during such tight markets as World War II, when employers "resorted" to hiring them for jobs men had previously held. Once employed in the new jobs, women have generally not retreated to the second line.

Since the 1940s women have not faced a serious downturn in demand for the jobs they typically perform. For the most part, declines have been in blue-collar jobs, while the white-collar and service jobs in which women have been concentrated have expanded.[4] Primary and secondary schoolteaching has only recently suffered a downturn. What happens to the male-female mix of professors if the market for higher education continues to soften? Have women applicants for academic posts advanced in the queue to the point where they compete with their male colleagues on the basis of their individual capabilities?

The problem of job shortage in academia has led to a reduction in graduate enrollments, as well as fewer faculty appointments. Alice Rossi shows how sharp the "string of change" will be for men if they must confront both a reduction in the total number of doctoral students being accepted and an improvement in the proportion of women in that total. Starting with a hypothetical total of 100 graduate students, 80 of whom are male and 20 female, she points out that a decline of 40 percent in the total number can be achieved by either of two ways: reducing each group to 40 percent, leaving women at 12 and men at 48; or increasing the number of women to 24, which would require that men's enrollment be cut to 36, or by 55 percent. "We should be extremely cautious not to dampen the legitimate aspirations of our competent women students," she notes, "but we must at the same time warn them about discouragement from men and the sources of men's response."[5]

Further evidence of women's higher job expectations, and a possible mismatch between these expectations and the jobs available in the economy as a whole, can be drawn from the Herbert Parnes data. He shows that mature women are now in the labor force far more frequently than they expected to be in their earlier years. About two-fifths of the young women surveyed altered their plans for work before age thirty-five. Overwhelmingly, they moved in the direction of more jobs and longer worklives. Moreover, these revisions in plans are consistent with those currently exhibited by women in the 35 to 44 year age group, whose participation rates are 61 percent and 52 percent for black and white women, respectively.

In Parnes' study, women's plans for increased work are attributed to their reduced childbearing expectations and to the emphasis in recent years on women's liberation. Since the girls who were attending school during the period of the survey exhibited the greatest change in plans concerning work, educational influences seem to have played a significant role in forming family and work goals.

Occupational aspirations of the women are even more indicative of an increasing commitment to market careers. About three-quarters of the white and two-thirds of the black women indicated preferences for white-collar occupations, with fully half of the white-collar aspirants looking forward to work in professional, technical, or managerial jobs. These goals appear overly optimistic when compared with the performance of women now in the 35 to 44 year age group. Only 23 percent of the white and 14 percent of the black women employed as wage and salary workers are in professional or managerial positions. One concern is obvious: even with increasing educational attainment and expanded market opportunities for women, it seems doubtful that the aspirations of the younger women will be achieved. However, their stated goals illustrate that women not only expect to enter the workforce in increasing numbers, but also that they are aiming for higher-level positions than are currently being achieved by women workers. Additional evidence of the commitment of women to market work emerged in Parnes' survey of women who worked. About 65 percent of them reported that they would continue to work even if they could live comfortably without their market earnings.[6]

Academic Institutions

Turning from the economy as it affects the market for academic professional talent, what about the institutions that do the hiring? A policy of hiring faculty and staff on the basis of ability sounds equitable, nonsexist, completely fair, and in a period of talent shortage fine qualitative distinctions are unnecessary. However, in the years ahead competition will come to be much keener and the need for objective criteria far greater because there will be more men and women competing for each job. The difficulty of dismissing the issue with a casual reference to hiring based on ability springs from lack of agreement as to what constitutes ability. Institutions and individuals are quite ambivalent on matters of academic quality. Examination would probably reveal that tenured appointments are almost always given to persons with good (or at least long) publication lists, with some token nod to teaching ability, however, measured, and other campus activities. The problem is compounded in offering the first appointment, since neither teaching nor research ability may have been demonstrated.

There can be little doubt that in the past most women have tended to give teaching their primary attention and that men have published more frequently. Since research has been more handsomely rewarded, men's academic records have been more impressive. We may protest—and often do—that these priorities are inappropriate. As long as they remain the institutions' priorities, those who march to different drummers march at the end of the line. The fact that a teaching emphasis has been more prevalent among women means that women have moved up through the ranks more slowly. However, the sex difference in publication record may narrow among the assistant professors of the future, as young career-oriented women come to accept the research criteria for promotion and tenure. Quite possibly too, there may be some shift in emphasis that will offer greater rewards to teaching quality.

If quality were clearly specified, an institution would find it very difficult to defend hiring one sex in preference of the other, or paying salary differentials for the same job. Sex differences in earnings could persist, however, if there is stereotyping of jobs, with males being appointed as chairmen and administrators; or if women concentrate in certain disciplines, thereby overcrowding those markets and leaving the sciences, engineering, and economics to men. Expansion in the numbers of women in certain disciplines is essential if present affirmative action goals are to be met.

Even with a rapid growth in the numbers of women with doctorates, it is important to note that it will be several decades before the mix of males and females will approach 50-50. Elizabeth Scott estimates that if universities hired only women from 1970 to 182, the female proportion would reach almost 50 percent by 1982; and that a hiring pattern of 50 percent women would bring their proportion up to only about 30 percent by that time.[7],[a] Since it is clearly not appropriate to restrict hiring to women during the next several years, one conclusion is inevitable: men will continue to assume a majority of the academic posts for quite some time. The longer and more severe the depression in higher education, the slower will be the pace in changing the sex mix of university faculties.

However, we must not overlook the tremendous strides institutions have made in very recent years (never mind, for the moment, whether they did so because of pressure from HEW or NOW or some other acronym, or from a change of heart). A recent study from Allan Cartter shows that by 1973, discrimination against women in terms of the level of institution of their first job placement (in research, postdoctoral activity, or teaching appointment) had been eliminated. As evidence, he shows that in the 1967-1973 period the status of the institution to which the new woman doctorates went was as high or higher than the one from which she took her doctorate as often as such was the case for a new male doctorate.[8] Bayer and Astin have further concluded that salary discrimination against new women doctorates has also virtually disappeared.[9] Cartter concludes, therefore, that "equity at the point of entry to the job

[a]Assuming an initial mix of 15 percent women, 85 percent men, in 1969.

market—a critically necessary first step—had apparently been achieved in the academic arena by 1973."[10]

There are many other things the institutions can do to accommodate those women they have hired or will hire. The most obvious need is for part-time faculty arrangements that allow women to meet family responsibilities, but continue to progress in their professions. The practice of hiring women as lecturers and instructors to handle introductory courses has meant that these women usually

> ... are not privileged to vote in faculty meetings, nor are they eligible for the full range of faculty benefits, such as leaves, support for scholarship, tenure, and opportunity to participate in decision making. Marginal appointments, even if fulltime, carry one-year contracts, little possibility for promotion, little security, and almost no research stability.[11]

Demands for part-time working schedules are not peculiar to the academic profession, nor to women. Widespread discontent with work arrangements has attracted the nation's attention, resulting in many attempts to provide flexibility in the timing of work. In academic institutions there has been some pressure to lower retirement age or to offer phased retirement plans that include part-time teaching during the latter part of worklife. In a few instances married couples trained in the same discipline have asked to share an academic appointment (which probably means they would share domestic responsibilities as well).

In speculating on future institutional policies, it is well to remember that women, too, will have a voice in the formation of those policies. Whereas the numbers of women holding tenured posts and key administrative positions in institutions of higher education traditionally have been small, a decade of sustained improvement in their status should make a significant difference. The increasing frequency of women college presidents, university deans and provosts, and most important of all, the rapid rise in female enrollment in graduate schools, could have a profound influence on educational policy. If women academicians have different priorities than men—if teaching quality and student counseling appear more important, for example, to women—there will come to be more support for rewards based on teaching. Graduate study will be affected even earlier, if women perceive the relevant questions in their various disciplines to be somewhat different from those men choose to pursue. Indeed, it is interesting to speculate on the possible change in content of one's discipline— Which questions come to be asked? What areas of the subject assume priority?— as the numbers of women in the discipline increase.

There are broader questions of the direction of institutional change and the choices among alternative programs, as well as economic questions having to do with the merits of investments in various levels of education and the priorities between higher education and health or the environment, for example. These are questions for which the new breed of women educators will share responsibility. Since decision-making in the allocation of educational resources has not been a woman's role in the past, women have had little experience in dealing with such issues. The successes and failures of educational administration have been almost exclusively those of men.

However, in the last quarter of this century women will be helping to make major decisions in higher education, and we must have some perspective of where we want the "industry" to go. We must worry about total job placements, not just the needs of women; fellowship support for all graduate students, when public funds are being cut; institutional accountability; governance; and retirement annuities. The university of the year 2000 will be a different institution from the one that confers your degree in 1975, and women can influence markedly the changes that lie ahead.

Academic Women

Finally, then, what of today's academic woman? What can we say of her that has not been said too often and with too little evidence? One should observe first that the gifted, articulate, no-nonsense women coming out of today's graduate schools defy categorization. To drag out the labels pinned on academic women in the past is clearly inappropriate. Today's woman doctorate is not likely to be a spinster, as she once was; not necessarily eager to avoid competing with males; not limited to study of the humanities and social sciences; and not planning to limit her career to allow for time to raise a large family—indeed, she may not be planning to have children at all. The kinds of demands her career aspirations place on her; her husband and family, if any; and on the academy itself are important.

Note the contrast with the past, even the very recent past. From a study of women who received doctorates in 1950, 1960, and 1968, John Centra identifies four major types: one, women who have subsequently worked fulltime and made substantial contributions to their fields; two, the majority of women doctorates, who have pursued their careers all or part of the time, usually as teachers, but who have not been in the forefront of their professions; three, the 15 to 20 percent who have worked intermittently and on the periphery of their disciplines; and four, the 5 percent who have seldom used their graduate training professionally. "The award of the doctorate degree does not, by any means," he concludes, "anoint one with success or even ambition."[1][2]

In explaining this recent pattern on the basis of cultural tradition, expectations of men and women, and discrimination, the author points out that some changes are in the making. One change is in numbers. Women's proportion of Ph.D. and Ed.D. degrees rose from 13 percent in 1970, to 16 percent in 1972, and to 18 percent in 1973. Graduate enrollments are also higher. In the 208

Ph.D.-granting institutions in 1973, 37 percent of the graduate students were women. Another difference one may suspect, although not yet documented, lies in the change in attitude toward women graduate students on the part of professors, male students, and the women themselves. Comments by women receiving degrees in earlier years reveal the difficulties they faced from lack of sponsorship or even acceptance by professors, disparagement of women's scholarly capacities, and obvious discrimination in hiring.[13] One wonders whether these blatant practices are prevalent today and if so, whether complaints are being lodged. Granted that discrimination can take many forms, some quite subtle and difficult to demonstrate. Nevertheless, it appears that the more recent women students are finding fewer instances of overt discrimination. As for hiring policy, the complaints deal chiefly with the job shortage rather than any discernible preference for men doctorates.

Today's wider acceptance of women in academic posts and other professions is somewhat similar to the breakthroughs achieved during the Second World War, when women moved rapidly into industrial jobs. In the early 1940s the need to have women join the work force prompted the change in practice, however, and there was no male competition for the positions. In the 1970s, jobs are scarce, particularly in academia; competition among women and men will be severe for quite some time. The jobs being sought, moreover, are those that call for career commitment and long years of preparation. There is one other important difference. In contrast to the women who were pulled into the labor force temporarily during the war effort, the woman doctorate today has been motivated by her own interests and aspirations and the expectation of a lifetime career.

It would be unwise to view the prospects of career fulfillment as guaranteed merely because of the greater acceptance of women professionals. Such acceptance is necessary but it is not sufficient. It is true, as Alice Rossi concludes, that "... the student who is female, white or black, will find doors open to her that typically were closed. There will be greater opportunities for women in academe as well as other sectors of the economy...."[14] The economy-wide decline in job opportunities must be reckoned within the short run, and the prospects of slower growth and its related restrictions on employment in the longer run. In this new academic era of steady state, equality of opportunity will be of enormous importance. In the absence of such equality women would have fewer chances for advancement than they have had in recent decades of high growth. It would also be a mistake for the married woman with children to underestimate the strain of a dual career, no matter how carefully planned and timed. It takes as much time to rear a child as it ever did—which is to say, as much time as one can give to it.

John Gardner has reminded us that a generation has no choice as to the challenges the forces of history throw in its lap. It has only the choice of how it will respond to those challenges. In your response to today's challenge you will of course find yourself concerned with scholarship and teaching and growing. You will also be involved, most of you, with your husbands and children and community responsibilities. To keep your perspective in a world in which there are too many exciting things to do and too little time to do them is not easy, nor is it ever dull.

It is perhaps easier to change the institutions—to open up the opportunities—than it is to find time to take advantage of them. For as sociologist Wilbert Moore has noted: "The only close rival of money as a pervasive and awkward scarcity is time." Because time is so scarce it is important that you enjoy the work itself. Otherwise, it is not worth the effort and the dedication academia demands of its women and men.

Notes

1. Margaret Mead's term, cited-in Jessie Bernard, *Academic Women* (University Park: Pennsylvania State University Press, 1964).

2. Ibid., p. 92.

3. See the author's "The Woman Professional in Higher Education," in W. Todd Furniss and Patricia A. Graham, *Women in Higher Education* (Washington, D.C.: American Council on Education, 1974), pp. 75-94.

4. Valerie Oppenheimer, *The Female Labor Force in the United States*, Population Monograph Series, No. 5 (Berkeley: University of California Press, 1970).

5. Alice Rossi, "Summary and Prospects," in Rossi, *Academic Women on the Move* (New York: Russell Sage Foundation, 1973).

6. Herbert Parnes, *Dual Careers*, Manpower Research Monograph No. 21, vol. 1 (Washington: U.S. Department of Labor, Manpower Administration, 1970).

7. See *Opportunities for Women in Higher Education*, Carnegie Commission on Higher Education (New York: McGraw-Hill, 1973), Appendix C, p. 231.

8. Allan Cartter and Wayne E. Ruhter, *The Disappearance of Sex Discrimination in First Job Placements of New Ph.D..s* (Los Angeles: Higher Education Research Institute, 1975).

9. Cited in Cartter and Ruhter, op. cit., from an article to be published in *Science* in 1975.

10. Ibid., p. 25.

11. Sheila Tobias and Margaret L. Rumbarger, "Rearrangements in Faculty Schedules," in Furniss and Graham, op. cit., p. 128.

12. John A. Centra, *Women, Men, and the Doctorate* (Princeton: Educational Testing Service, 1974), p. 162.

13. Ibid., pp. 185-213.

14. Rossi, op. cit., p. 527.

3

Recent Trends in the Employment of American Women

James A. Sweet

My task is to present, in limited form, the historical pattern of employment of women in the United States. This task is made even more difficult by the fact that it is impossible to consider employment trends in a vacuum, without also considering changes in other areas of the lives of women. I will confine myself primarily to *recent* trends in the employment of women and related activities, focusing on the post-World War II period and particularly the period since 1960.[1]

In March of 1973, 44 percent of all women aged 16 and over were in the labor force. This compares to a figure of 78 percent for men at the same date. There has been a more or less continuous rise in the employment rate of women during the last century. At about the turn of the century it is estimated that 20 percent of American women were in the labor force. By 1940, this figure had risen to about 26 percent. There was, following 1940, an acceleration in the trend; and, by 1950, 29 percent of women were in the labor force. A further acceleration began around 1955 when 31 percent of women were in the labor force. Five years later 34 percent were in the labor force, and, by 1965, 38 percent. In the eight years since 1965 the rate has risen to the present level of about 44 percent.

In addition to the rise in the absolute rate of employment, there have been very significant changes in the life cycle patterns of employment of American women. In his fascinating study contrasting work patterns of women around 1890 with those in the mid-twentieth century, Robert W. Smuts observes:

The typical 1890 working woman is easily sketched. She was young and single, the daughter of ambitious, hard-working, immigrants or native farmers. With little education or training, she was spending the years between school and marriage in one of the many kinds of unskilled jobs available in the city. The main variations from this type can also be readily discerned: widows, wives whose husbands did not support them, Negro women in farm or domestic service

Acknowledgements: The author's continuing research on the employment and earnings of women in the United States is supported by funds granted to the Institute for Research on Poverty at the University of Wisconsin by the Office of Economic Opportunity pursuant to the Economic Opportunity Act of 1964. The opinions expressed are solely those of the author. The research also benefitted from a research grant from NICHD (grant #HD02197). In addition, the data processing for this project benefitted greatly from the Population Research Center grant (5 Pol-HDO5876) awarded to the Center for Demography and Ecology at the University of Wisconsin by the Center for Population Research of NICHD.

jobs in the South, immigrant wives in the cotton mills of the North, and a few unconventional women who worked even though others in similar circumstances did not.[2]

Most of the married women who worked outside the home had little choice; they were the victims of one misfortune or another which deprived them of adequate support by a husband. The kinds of adversities which led wives to seek work are suggested by a study conducted by the U.S. Bureau of Labor Statistics in 1908. Among one group of 140 wives and widows who were employed in the glass industry, 94 were widows, or had been deserted, or were married to men who were permanently disabled. Thirteen were married to drunkards or loafers who would not work. The husbands of ten were temporarily unable to work because of sickness or injury. Seventeen were married to unskilled laborers who received minimum wages for uncertain employment. Only six were married to regularly employed workers above the grade of unskilled labor.[3]

In Figure 3-1, we have plotted the age patterns of employment for birth cohorts of women. By birth cohorts, we mean the women who were born in the year indicated. For example, the lowest line, which is labeled "1886-1890" shows the labor force participation rate at ages 30-34 through 55-59 for women who were born in the years between 1886 and 1890. Such women were first observed at age 30-34 in the 1920 census; they were observed ten years later in the 1930 census at ages 40-44, in the 1940 census at ages 50-54, and in the 1950 census at ages 60-64. We have no measurement for this cohort at younger ages since we do not have reliable estimates of labor force participation rates before 1920. The first cohort for which we have complete information is the 1896-1900 cohort. This cohort shows a drop in employment between ages 20-24, 25-29, and 30-34, and then a slow rise in employment from ages 30-34 through ages 55-59. The later cohorts show the same characteristic pattern of decline at the marriage and childbearing ages. Each successive cohort shows a steeper rise in the ages in the thirties and forties. Of course, we do not have the labor force experience at the older ages for the most recent cohorts because they have not yet reached those ages.

Notice that there is very little difference in rates at ages 20-24 for the cohorts between 1906-1910 and 1936-1940. There is then a sharp jump in the rate of employment for women 20-24 for the cohort 1946-1950 and for the 1950-1954 cohort whose rate we have estimated as being about 62 percent at ages 20-24. There has been a very marked change in age pattern of employment, with more recent cohorts having sharper rises at the ages over 30 and the two most recent cohorts having much higher rates in ages 20-24 and for the 1946-1950 cohort at ages 25-29. These last two cohorts are ones that have participated in the low fertility pattern characteristic of the 1970s.

In Figure 3-2, we show labor force participation patterns for women at different life cycle stages as of 1973. In contrast to the patterns shown in Figure 3-1, Figure 3-2 does not represent the experience of an actual group of women

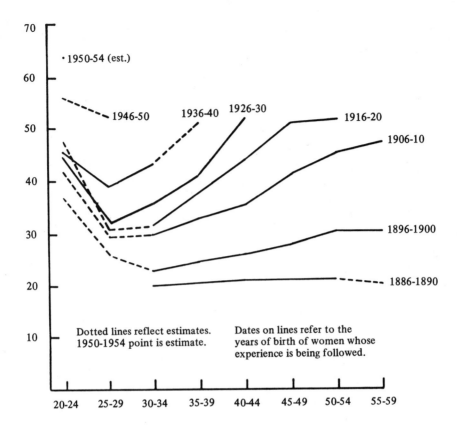

Source: J.A. Sweet, *Women in the Labor Force* (New York: Seminar, 1973), pp. 58-60; and U.S. Bureau of Labor Statistics, Special Labor Force Report #164, "Marital and Family Characteristics of the Labor Force, March 1973."

Figure 3-1. Age Patterns of Employment for Birth Cohorts of Women

living through their life cycle, but rather it takes the synthetic experience of women in various stages of the life cycle as of 1973, and looks at it as if it represented women moving through the life cycle. The classification in Figure 3-2 is mutually exclusive but is not exhaustive of the universe. What we have done is to attempt to show the most typical life cycle patterns experienced by American women. For example, a woman who remains single through her life cycle goes down the path shown in the left column of the figure, which shows the rates for single women at different ages. The modal pattern would be for a woman to marry in her late teens or twenties and live for a short time (one or two years) with no children; then to have a child in her early twenties; and then

28

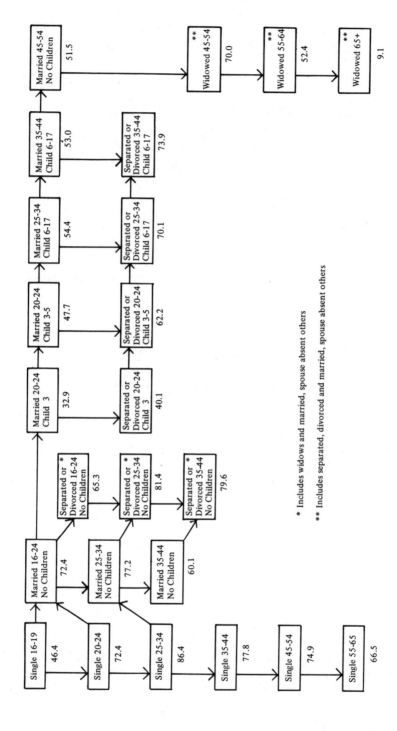

Source: U.S. Bureau of Labor Statistics, Special Labor Force Report #164, "Marital and Family Characteristics of the Labor Force, March 1973."

Figure 3-2. Synthetic Life Cycle of Labor Force Participation Patterns: 1973

* Includes widows and married, spouse absent others

** Includes separated, divorced and married, spouse absent others the woman ages as her family is built and subsequently her youngest child ages as the woman herself grows older. In that pattern we see that a woman who is single at age 16-19 (she is probably also in school) has a probability of employment of 46 percent; a woman who is single at age 20-24 has a rate of employment of 72 percent. If she marries and is without children for a period of time, the rate of employment remains at about 72 percent. If she marries at an older age and/or if she remains childless for a period of time, her employment rate is somewhat higher than this. As the married woman 16-24 with no children has her first child, she enters the status of being married with a child under three at age 20-24 and her employment rate is reduced substantially to approximately 33 percent. Other alternative patterns shown in the figure include a pattern involving a woman with young children experiencing separation and/or divorce (shown in the third column of the figure for childless women and shown in the lower row of the figure on the right side for women with children). Finally, we show the experience of widows in the right column of the figure.

Marriage, Fertility, and Education Trends

It is impossible to think about the changing patterns of employment of American women without at the same time considering changing marriage and reproductive patterns. The birth rate in the United States is at an all-time low. We have been experiencing continuous fertility declines since 1957. In Table 3-1, we show the crude birth rate and the general fertility rate for the United States starting in 1945 through 1973 (the general fertility rate is a summary measure of a population's fertility, adjusting in a rather crude way for changing population age distribution). The period from about 1948 to 1958 was a period of very high "baby boom" fertility. The crude birth rate during that decade ranged between 24 and 25. Between 1957 and 1967, the crude birth rate declined by approximately 30 percent from 25 to about 18. The crude rate stayed in the range 17 or 18 for the next four years until 1971. Then, a more rapid decrease began in 1971—declining to 15 in 1973 (for an additional 18 percent decline from the 1970 rate). Thus, between 1957 and 1973 the crude birth rate showed a total decline of more than 41 percent (the general fertility rate declined during this period by a total of 44 percent).

In understanding the fertility decline that has occurred and its implications, it is important not only to have a quantitative picture of fertility change but also a more qualitative sense of what happened and how it happened. In order to provide such a qualitative description in a very brief period, we must paint a very general picture without providing a great deal of detail or documentation.[4] What we will do is to compare several features of our reproductive life as they existed in the period, patterns in 1955 or 1960, with the situation in 1975. We will then

Table 3-1
Recent Trends in U.S. Fertility

Year[a]	Crude Birth Rate	General Fertility Rate
1945	20.4	85.9
1946	24.1	101.9
1947	26.6	113.3
1948	24.9	107.3
1949	24.5	107.1
1950	24.1	106.2
1951	24.9	111.5
1952	25.1	113.9
1953	25.1	115.2
1954	25.3	118.1
1955	25.0	118.5
1956	25.2	121.2
1957	25.3	122.9
1958	24.6	120.2
1959	24.3	120.2
1960	23.7	118.0
1961	23.3	117.2
1962	22.4	112.2
1963	21.7	108.5
1964	21.0	105.0
1965	19.4	96.6
1966	18.4	91.3
1967	17.8	87.6
1968	17.5	85.7
1969	17.7	85.8
1970	18.2	87.6
1971	17.3	82.3
1972	15.6	73.4
1973	15.0	69.3

[a]1959 and prior adjusted for underregistration of births. This change has an effect of 0.3 on the 1959 crude rate and 0.8 on the 1959 GFR.

Source: Vital Statistics Rates in the U.S.: 1940-1960, U.S. Public Health Service publication #1677; Vital Statistics of the U.S.: 1966, vol. I, Natality; Monthly Vital Statistics Report: Births, Marriages, Divorces and Deaths for 1973 (vol. 22, #12); Annual Summary for the U.S., 1972 (vol. 21, #13).

turn our attention to some possible reasons for the changes observed in our reproductive behavior. Couples reproducing in the 1950s were reproducing at a rate of more than three children per married couple. At the present time, couples are reproducing approximately two children. We will, of course, not know the ultimate average number of children for actual cohorts of women reproducing in the 1970s for some time.

Up until about 1960, American reproductive behavior was characterized by a number of features.

1. We married at very young ages, both by historical and cross-national standards. The median age at first marriage for women was about 20 years, and even for the college educated women the median age at first marriage was only about 22 years.

2. We tended to begin reproduction very soon after marriage. In approximately one-quarter of the cases, women's first birth was a pregnancy that began prior to the time of their first marriage and the median interval between marriage and the birth of the first child was approximately one year. A substantial share of couples—probably a majority—wanted to have their first child as soon as possible after their marriage.

3. There was a concentration of family size ideals in the two- to four-child range with considerably more persons reporting four-child ideal family size than two-child ideal family size. In terms of the number of children desired[a] by married couples, approximately 30 percent desired two children; 25 percent, three children; and 28 percent, four children.

4. Contraception was practiced in virtually all marriages during this period, but it was practiced somewhat infrequently and quite unsuccessfully for childspacing purposes. We tended to have very short birth intervals until the desired two, three, or four children were born.

5. The ability to control fertility tended to improve once desired family size was reached. However, there was a substantial number of accidental pregnancies and unwanted babies. In the period 1960-1965, approximately 20 percent of births were unwanted births in the sense that they were conceptions that occurred after the couple had had its last wanted child. Of people who were completing their reproduction in the mid-1960s, fully 31 percent had had number failures, that is, they had had more babies than they had wanted to

---

[a]Ideal family size refers to the answer to the following question: "What do you think is the ideal number of children for the average American family?" Desired family size is determined by the answer to a series of questions: "Q. 6: How many children do you have? Those who answered 'None' were asked Q. 10: If you could have exactly the number of children you want, what number would that be? All other respondents were asked: Q. 7: Have you had all the children you want? Those who answered 'No' to Question 7 were asked Q. 9: What number of children would you really have? Those who answered 'Yes' to Question 7 were asked: Q. 8: Would you just as soon have had fewer?" (Ryder and Westoff, *Reproduction in the United States, 1965*, Princeton University Press, 1971, pp. 26-27).

have,[b] and an additional 50 percent or so had had at least one timing failure, i.e., they had had at least one of their births too soon.

6. This high level of unwanted or poorly timed fertility may have been, at least in part, inherent in the contraceptive technology available and the methods of contraception that were used. The dominant methods of contraception during the period of 1955-1960 were condoms, used by approximately 27 percent of contraceptive married couples; diaphragm, used by approximately 25 percent; and the rhythm method, used by approximately 22 percent. An additional 7 percent were relying on withdrawal and 8 percent on douche.

The average age at which women were having their last wanted birth was about 25. In many cases, their last wanted birth occurred when the woman was in her early twenties. Thus women were left with a period of about twenty years of risk of conception prior to menopause with a selection of contraception that was not very reliable.

In the span of the last ten or fifteen years there has been a rather dramatic shift in reproductive behavior. By 1975:

1. There has apparently been a major shift in reproductive values. Ideal family size reported by women in the reproductive ages has shifted from a modal value of four children in 1960 to a modal value of two children by 1970 and from an average value of approximately 3.5 children to an average value of approximately 2.5 children. Among couples with wives, age 18-24, there has been a decline in average expected completed family size from 2.9 in 1967 to 2.2 in 1974.[5]

2. There has been a rapid change in the age at first marriage. We will document this later in this chapter.

3. There may well have been a decline in the prevalence of marriages "forced" by premarital pregnancy, although it is difficult to document this change in a convincing way.

4. There has been a dramatic shift in contraceptive technology as well as in birth control practice. The pill was introduced on the U.S. market as a contraceptive in 1960 and diffused very rapidly. The interuterine device was also introduced and has been diffusing particularly after 1965. As we have already pointed out, nearly three-quarters of the contraception in the period 1955-1960 was the diaphragm, condom, or rhythm method. By 1970, only about one-quarter of the contraception involved these methods. Thirty-four percent of women were pill users in 1970 and 16 percent of the women or their husbands had been sterilized in order to prevent further births. By the present time, perhaps one-third of couples who had had their last wanted birth had had a sterilization operation. This change in the type of birth control methods used has been a shift: (a) from relatively ineffective, to quite highly effective methods of birth control; (b) from methods that require some specific action be taken at the time of sexual intercourse, to methods which are unrelated to sexual activity

---

[b]For each pregnancy, women were asked retrospectively whether, at the time they became pregnant, they wanted to have another child at some time.

at all; and (c) from methods that require some specific action to avoid becoming pregnant to methods which tend to require that a woman or couple make some definite decision to get pregnant, i.e., to stop the pill taking routine or to have the IUD removed.

5. Throughout the United States, women have access to abortion, and abortion has become a much more acceptable and open thing than it was in the past. We have no idea what impact availability of legal abortion has had on the birth rate since we do not know the prevalence of illegal abortions prior to the liberalization of abortion laws. One might suspect however that there are relatively fewer forced marriages, there are relatively fewer illegitimate births, and there are relatively fewer unwanted children, i.e., number failures, than there would have been in the absence of the liberalization of abortion laws.[6]

6. Contraception early in marriage for childspacing purposes has become both more common and more effective. Nearly three-quarters of contraceptive young couples are using the birth control pill. Two-fifths of women married before age twenty used birth control within their marriage before their first pregnancy. Ten years ago, the figure was approximately 30 percent. Sixty-five percent of women married at age 20-24 used birth control prior to their first pregnancy in comparison to about 40 percent a decade ago.[7]

7. The childless and one-child marriage are likely to become more common, although there is no indication that this will be the modal reproductive pattern. There has been a rise from less than 1 percent to approximately 5 percent in the proportion of young married couples who expect to have no children at all and a rise from approximately 5 percent to approximately 15 percent in the proportion of young married couples who expect to have only one child.

Why has the decline in American reproductive patterns occurred? We have no definitive answer to this question, but a number of possible candidates are available, all of which probably have at least some validity for some groups within the population.

1. The decline in fertility has been simply a result of the improvement of birth control technology. This explanation is found wanting at least in its simplest form as the major explanation for fertility declines. First of all, there has clearly been a change in reproductive values. Secondly, in a number of European countries with very low fertility the "modern" methods of contraception have diffused very slowly and yet there is fertility as low or lower than that found in the United States. In addition, the very low fertility in the United States in the 1930s was achieved without the modern technology.[8]

2. Reproductive values may have changed as a result of changes elsewhere in our society. The rapid decline of fertility following 1970 is temporally correlated quite closely with the environmental movement which achieved great publicity and following during this period. Similarly, the women's movement was very active during this same period. Women are receiving the message that they may legitimately aspire to adult roles other than, or, in addition to, those

of wife and mother. As people came to see the old pattern of reproduction to be in conflict with environmental goals and in conflict with the goal of women achieving their full potential in other spheres of life people may have adapted their reproductive patterns.

3. Bumpasss has argued that changes in reproductive values may in part have been a response to changes in birth control technology.[9] He suggests that high fertility values may have been simply a rationalization of the inevitable, i.e., it made no sense to aspire to a one- or two-child family when the nature of birth control technology made the frustration of such aspirations more likely than their achievement.

4. The fertility decline following 1970 may be simply a short-run adaptation to a situation of economic adversity and uncertainty. This argument would imply that if and when the economy straightens itself out and the rate of inflation and the rate of unemployment both decline, the birth rate will increase.

5. Easterlin and others have proposed a more long-run economic explanation, arguing that persons spending their formative years in a relatively prosperous environment set a higher minimum acceptable material standard of living for themselves and consequently with other features of the material standard of living.[10]

6. Another factor is that the rising age at marriage and the apparent increase in attempts at, and success in, controlling fertility for child-spacing purposes early in marriage tend to reduce ultimate completed family size. To the extent that women have had work experience prior to marriage and between marriage and the birth of their first child, they become somewhat different people and their marriage becomes a somewhat different phenomenon than otherwise. Such women will be more likely to develop a self-image that is not dominated by motherhood and the maternal role.

In addition, they and their husbands are likely to have developed a standard of living that is dependent on two incomes. It therefore becomes much more expensive to leave the work force to have a child in terms of foregone earnings, and much more of a hassle if the woman chooses to continue working full-time and to take on what is essentially a full-time job as mother. Consequently, first and subsequent births are likely to be delayed more, and there is likely to be a reassessment of fertility goals and smaller ultimate family size.

The decline in fertility, described in the aggregate, pervades all segments of our society. In Table 3-2, we show fertility change measures between 1957-1960 and 1967-1970 for a number of racial and ethnic subgroups, as well as for the urban white and rural farm population. The declines are found to be present for all subgroups and to be particularly large for those racial and ethnic minorities that previously had unusually high fertility, e.g., Southern rural blacks.

Within the urban white population, the decline in fertility described is also pervasive. It is found for women with high levels of education and also for those with less than a high school education. It is found for wives of high income men

Table 3-2
Duration Standardized Recent Fertility Rates

| | 1960 | | 1970 | | % Change | | Relative Level (Urban White = 1.000) | | | |
| | | | | | | | Crude | | Standard | |
	Crude	Standard	Crude	Standard	Crude	Standard	1960	1970	1960	1970
Blacks										
Southern Rural	.803	.824	.515	.515	35.9	37.5	1.52	1.29	1.56	1.33
Southern Urban	.644	.637	.433	.406	32.8	36.3	1.22	1.09	1.20	1.05
Nonsouth	.598	.593	.414	.390	30.8	34.2	1.13	1.04	1.12	1.01
Japanese American	.553	.451	.385	.352	30.3	22.0	1.05	0.97	0.85	0.91
Chinese American	.550	.523	.425	.389	22.7	25.6	1.04	1.07	0.99	1.01
Puerto Rican American[a]	.634	.568	.521	.465	17.8	18.1	1.20	1.31	1.07	1.20
Mexican American[a]	.798	.779	.568	.548	28.8	29.7	1.51	1.43	1.47	1.42
Spanish Surname[b]	.775	.768	.550	.537	29.0	30.1	1.47	1.38	1.45	1.39
Urban White	.529	.529	.398	.387	24.8	26.8	1.00	1.00	1.00	1.00
Rural Farm	.581	.636	.393	.469	32.4	26.3	1.10	0.99	1.20	1.21

[a]Definitions differ between 1960 and 1970. Change measures are therefore not strictly correct. For 1960 these groups include first and second generation Mexican Americans and Puerto Rican Americans. For 1970, they include persons who report themselves as being of Mexican or Puerto Rican descent.

[b]Spanish Surname in 5 Southwestern States.

Note: Standardized on 1960 Urban White Marriage Duration Distribution

Source: J.A. Sweet, "Recent Fertility Change among High Fertility Minorities in the U.S.," Working Paper 74-11, Center for Demography and Ecology, University of Wisconsin-Madison, 1974. Reprinted with permission of the Center for Demography and Ecology, University of Wisconsin.

as well as for wives of lower income men. It is found in all regions of the country, for the metropolitan and nonmetropolitan, rural and urban populations.[11]

The age at marriage distribution of American women has been changing. The U.S. experienced a long period of declining age at marriage. During the mid-1960s the trend in age at marriage began to reverse itself. Table 3-3 shows the magnitude of these changes as of 1972. In 1960, 46 percent of 20-year-old women had never been married, while by 1972, 59 percent had never been married. This increase in marriage ages pervades all groups including the well-educated as well as poorly educated, blacks as well as whites.

At this point, it is not possible to know whether there is going to be an increase in the proportion of cohorts that never marry, an increase in the proportion whose first marriages occur at ages 25 or more, or whether the change will simply be an upward shift of a year or so in the whole marriage function. Whatever ultimately happens, any upward shift in the age at first marriage is likely to be significant.

We know that there is a large and persisting fertility differential between women marrying in their teens, women marrying at age 20-21, and women marrying beyond age 21.

We know that women who work between school and marriage and between

Table 3-3
Percent of Women Single, by Age: 1972 and 1960

Age	1972	1960	Change[a]
18 years	83.0	75.6	7.4
19 years	70.7	59.7	11.0
20 years	59.0	46.0	13.0
21 years	44.3	34.6	9.7
22 years	36.3	25.6	10.7
23 years	25.3	19.4	5.9
24 years	17.4	15.7	1.7
25 years	17.5	13.1	4.4
26 years	13.9	11.4	2.5
27 years	11.3	10.2	1.1
28 years	9.5	9.2	0.3
29 years	8.2	8.7	−0.5

[a]Differences shown were derived by using rounded percentages for 1972 and 1960.
Source: U.S. Bureau of the Census, Current Population Reports, "Marital Status & Living Arrangements: March 1972," Series P-20, No. 242 (Washington, D.C.: U.S. Government Printing Office, 1972), Table E, p. 4.

marriage and first birth tend to have higher employment rates later in life than those who did not.

Women who spend time liberated from dependence on their families of orientation prior to marriage are likely to develop a greater sense of independence and self-sufficiency and a rather different self-image than persons who move immediately from a dependent relationship in their family of orientation to a similar dependent relationship in a family of procreation.[12]

Any analysis of employment patterns of women must take into account both the supply and demand side. On the supply side we must keep in mind the fact that as a result of the baby boom, there is a larger number of young women in the early reproductive ages, say 18-24, in the late 1960s than there were in the early 1960s or late 1950s. This is the case because the birth cohorts of 1947 and later were considerably larger than earlier birth cohorts. Consequently, there are more women competing for jobs than there would have been, had the baby boom not occurred. A complete picture would also include the fact that there are more young men competing with these young women for employment opportunities as well.

Table 3-4 shows the total number of women, age 18-24, between 1950 and 1973. During the 1950s, there were approximately 7.5 to 8 million women in these ages. Between 1960 and 1963, the number increased from 8 to 9 million; between 1963 and 1966 there was an increase from 9 to 10.5 million; and between 1966 and 1973 the total number grew to over 13 million women age 18 to 24. This growth in the size of the cohort, age 18-24, is important to our discussion of patterns of employment because employment at these ages is very high and these ages constitute labor force entry ages for the majority of women—both women completing high school as well as women completing college education. Thus the increase in rates of employment is even more impressive, given the rapid growth in the supply of female workers, as well as a corresponding increase in the supply of young male workers.

It is also important to realize that the 1960s was a period of continued growth in the educational attainment of American women. Seventy-five percent of women, age 22-24, in 1960 who had begun high school had gone on to complete it. By 1970, this proportion for the same age group was 85 percent. Similarly, among those who were high school graduates in 1960, 32 percent of the women had begun college by age 22-24 whereas by 1970 this proportion had increased to 43 percent. Among women, age 25-29, in 1960 who had begun college, 41 percent had completed college, while by 1970 the figure had risen to 47 percent. This is not to say that the educational attainment of women had achieved parity with that of men. The rates for men were also increasing, but the gap between men and women in college attendance and completion has narrowed. What we are emphasizing here, however, is that there has been a rather significant shift in educational achievements of women in this decade, which has an impact on their employment patterns.[13] (See Table 3-5.)

Table 3-4
Number of Women, Age 18-24, in the United States: 1950-1973 (Thousands)

Year	Number of Women
1950	8,057
1951	7,887
1952	7,721
1953	7,606
1954	7,526
1955	7,465
1956	7,471
1957	7,521
1958	7,624
1959	7,799
1960	8,018
1961	8,452
1962	8,795
1963	9,086
1964	9,338
1965	10,058
1966	10,590
1967	11,050
1968	11,322
1969	11,737
1970	12,247
1971	12,800
1972	12,868
1973	13,105

Sources: U.S. Bureau of the Census, Current Population Reports, "Estimates of the Population of the United States, by Single Years of Age, Color, and Sex: 1900 to 1959," Series P-25, No. 311 (Washington, D.C.: U.S. Government Printing Office, 1965); U.S. Bureau of the Census, Current Population Reports, "Estimates of the Population of the United States, by Age, Sex, and Race: April 1, 1960 to July 1, 1973," Series P-25, No. 519 (Washington, D.C.: U.S. Government Printing Office, 1974); U.S. Bureau of the Census, Current Population Reports, "Estimates of the Population of the United States, by Age, Sex, and Race: July 1, 1974 and April 1, 1970," Series P-25, No. 529 (Washington, D.C.: U.S. Government Printing Office, 1974).

Employment Trends

Figure 3-3 shows data from the Current Population Survey reports on employment of married women by presence and age of children. Some of the series go back as far as 1952, while others begin in 1959. There was a rapid increase in the

Table 3-5
Rates of Continuation in School, by Age and Sex: 1960 and 1970

	7-8		8-9		9-12		12-13		13-16		16-17+	
	1970	1960	1970	1960	1970	1960	1970	1960	1970	1960	1970	1960
Females												
16-17	984	965	960	938								
18-19	987	972	980	956	676	638						
20-21	987	970	978	951	862	755	456	338				
22-24	983	962	974	941	851	754	434	320	395	363		
25-29	979	950	965	927	816	743	385	307	471	406	273	189
30-34	970	939	952	910	788	731	338	313	448	412	285	231
Males												
16-17	974	940	934	903								
18-19	983	956	976	940	610	575						
20-21	981	956	974	932	858	746	546	420				
22-24	978	945	968	920	866	758	508	425	399	381		
25-29	972	931	957	904	835	756	490	455	541	531	484	402
30-34	959	916	938	878	809	715	456	471	577	580	510	429

Note: The conditional probability of moving from education level X to $(X+1)$. I.e., of women 22-24 in 1970, 851 of 1000 who completed grade 9, have gone on to complete grade 12.

Sources: For 1960: U.S. Bureau of the Census, "U.S. Census of Population: 1960, Subject Reports, Educational Attainment," Final Report PC(2)-5B (Washington, D.C.: U.S. Government Printing Office, 1963). For 1970: U.S. Bureau of the Census, "U.S. Census of Population: 1970, Subject Reports, Educational Attainment," Final Report PC(2)-5B (Washington, D.C.: U.S. Government Printing Office, 1973).

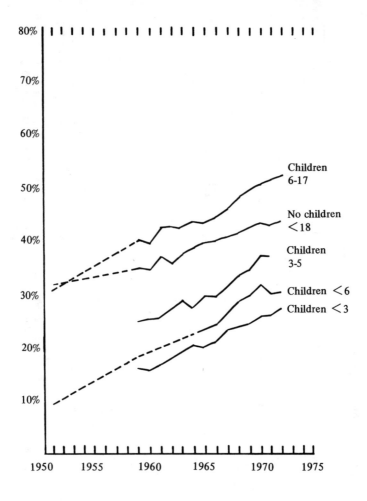

Source: See Table 3-6.

Figure 3-3. Labor Force Participation Rates of Married Women, Spouse Present, by Presence of Children: 1951-1972

rate of employment of all categories of women. During the period from 1959 to 1974, the employment rate of mothers with children under the age of three more than doubled, rising from approximately 15 percent to approximately 31 percent—a rise of 16 percentage points in a fifteen-year period, or approximately 1 percentage point per year (see Table 3-6). Mothers of children, age 3-5, had a similar pattern of increase with a rise from approximately 25 to approximately 39 percent—a rise of 14 points in the fifteen-year period. This trend during the 1960s was at approximately the same rate as the trend between 1950 and 1960.

Table 3-6

Labor Force Participation Rates of Married Women, Husband Present, by Presence and Age of Children: March 1960-1974

| | All Wives | No Children Under 18 Years | With Children under 18 Years | | | Under 6 Years | |
			Total	6 to 17 Years only	Total	3 to 5 Years none under 3 Years	Under 3 Years
1960	30.5	34.7	27.6	39.0	18.6	25.1	15.3
1961	32.7	37.3	29.6	41.7	20.0	25.5	17.0
1962	32.7	36.1	30.3	41.8	21.3	27.2	18.2
1963	33.7	37.4	31.2	41.5	22.5	28.5	19.4
1964	34.4	37.8	32.0	40.3	22.7	26.7	20.5
1965	34.7	38.3	32.2	42.7	23.3	29.2	20.0
1966	35.4	38.4	33.2	43.7	24.2	29.1	21.2
1967	36.8	38.9	35.3	45.0	26.5	31.7	23.3
1968	38.3	40.1	36.9	46.9	27.6	34.0	23.4
1969	39.6	41.0	38.6	48.6	28.5	34.7	24.2
1970	40.8	42.2	39.7	49.2	30.3	37.0	25.8
1971	40.8	42.1	39.7	49.4	29.6	36.1	25.7
1972	41.5	42.7	40.5	50.2	30.1	36.1	26.9
1973	42.2	42.8	41.7	50.1	32.7	38.3	29.4
1974	43.0	43.0	43.1	51.2	34.4	39.1	31.0

Source: For 1973: U.S. Bureau of Labor Statistics, Special Labor Force Report #164, "Marital and Family Characteristics of the Labor Force, March 1973," Tables F and I (Washington, D.C.: U.S. Government Printing Office, 1973). For earlier years: annual Special Labor Force Reports #2, 7, 20, 26, 40, 50, 55, 64, 80, 99, 120, 130, 144, 157, and Current Population Reports, Series P-50, #5, 11, 22, 25, 39, 44, 50, 62, 73, 76, 81, and 87.

The employment rates of mothers of older children, age 6-17, rose by about 10 points during the same period from a base of 40 percent, while the rate for married women with no children under the age of 18 rose from approximately 35 percent to 43 percent—a rise of 8 points, or about one-half point per year.

This latter group of women with no children under the age of 18 is a very heterogeneous group comprising women who have just married and who may be working prior to the birth of their first child, women who are and will remain childless through their lives, and older women whose children have grown up and left the parental household. We find quite different trends for the different groups as shown in Figure 3-4. For the youngest group—women, age 14-24— we find a rise in employment between 1959 and 1972 from approximately 58 percent to approximately 70 percent—a rise again of about 1 percentage point

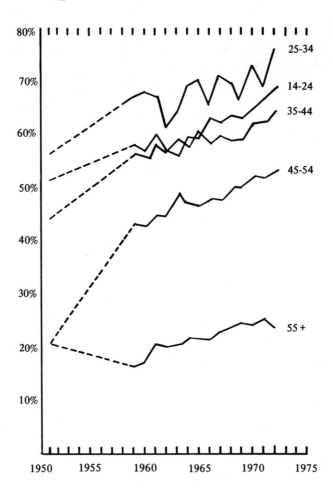

Source: See Table 3-6.

Figure 3-4. Labor Force Participation Rates of Married Women, Spouse Present, by Age, with No Children Under 18 Present: 1951-1972

per year. Most of this rise is concentrated in the period 1963 to 1972. Childless women, age 25-34, have roughly the same pattern although since their numbers are smaller, the interannual fluctuations are greater (due largely to sampling unreliability) with a rise from 65 percent to approximately 75 percent by 1972. The older women, age 55 and older, had relatively slower rises in their employment rates of about one-half point per year during this period.

In addition to the fact that fewer women are giving birth to children each year, there is an important change in the employment behavior of women who do give birth to a child. It is not easy to make precise comparisons, but we have estimated that there has been an increase in the probability of employment during pregnancy and probably a growth in the proportion of women working later into their pregnancies.[14] These estimates are based on data for the period of time that precedes the change in the legislation affecting employment of women during pregnancy. With the introduction of this legislation in April 1972, the Equal Employment Opportunity Commission, the agency that enforces Title VII of the Civil Rights Act of 1964, published amended Guidelines on Discrimination Because of Sex stating that: (1) employers may not exclude from employment applicants or employees because of pregnancy, and (2) pregnancy disabilities must be treated like other temporary disabilities.

Disabilities caused or contributed to by pregnancy, miscarriage, abortion, childbirth, and recovery therefrom are for all job-related purposes, temporary disabilities and should be treated as such under any health or temporary disability insurance or sick leave plan available in connection with employment. Written and unwritten employment policies and practices involving matters such as the commencement and duration of leave, the availability of extensions, the accrual of seniority and other benefits and privileges, reinstatement, and payment under any health or temporary disability insurance or sick leave plan, formal or informal, shall be applied to disability due to pregnancy or childbirth on the same terms and conditions as they are applied to other temporary disabilities.
    Where the termination of an employee who is temporarily disabled is caused by an employment policy under which insufficient or no leave is available, such a termination violates the Act if it has a disparate impact on employees of one sex and is not justified by business necessity.

Similar guidelines have been issued pursuant to a number of state laws, covering some employers not covered by the federal legislation. Such guidelines will not permit the continuation of employers' formal or informal practices or clauses in collective bargaining agreements that required pregnant women to leave their jobs (as, for example, in the Wisconsin retail clerks' contract) by the sixth month of pregnancy, and to remain away from their jobs for two months after delivery. Employment rates during the later months of pregnancy will undoubtedly increase still further.[15]

In another paper, we were able to document that women return to work after childbirth in higher proportions and earlier in recent years than they did earlier. At the time of the 1970 census, 18 percent of the women with a child under the age of 12 months; 23 percent of women with a child, age 12-23 months; and 27 percent of women with a youngest child, age 24-35 months, were employed at the time of the census. These figures compare with 10, 17, and 19 percent, respectively, for 1960. Thus, between 1960 and 1970 the rate of employment of women with children under the age of one rose by more than 80 percent, while the rates for women with youngest child, age 1 and 2, rose by approximately 40 percent.[16]

Making use of data contained in the census on year last worked as well as work experience during the previous year, we were able to decompose rates of current employment for women with a child, age 12-23.9 months, into four multiplicative components. The current employment rate of such women equals the product of: (a) the proportion of women who have ever worked in their lives, (b) the conditional probability that a woman who has ever worked has recent work experience, (c) the conditional probability that a woman with recent work experience has returned since the birth of her most recent child, and (d) the conditional probability that a woman who has returned to work since the birth of her child is still working at the time of the census. In 1970, 87 percent of women with a child, age 12-23.9 months, had worked. Of them, 84 percent had had work experience prior to the most recent birth. Of them, 54 percent have returned to work since the birth of their most recent child, and of them 61 percent were still working at the time of enumeration in the census. Compared with 1960, all four components have increased.[c]

An investigation of differentials in rates of returning to work shows that: (a) women with high levels of education have higher rates of returning to work, (b) women whose husbands have low to middle incomes have higher rates of return to work than do women whose husbands have middle to high incomes, and (c) black women have much higher rates of return to employment than white women (82 percent vs. 52 percent).

We found differences in rates of remaining at work. Women have higher probabilities of remaining at work after having returned to work: (a) if they have very high levels of education, (b) if they are black, and (c) if they are older than average. There are very little differences in rates of remaining at work in relation to husband's income or the number of children born previously.

Differentials in Employment Rates

In the past decade there have been a great number of empirical studies of the labor force behavior of American women. Studies of employment differentials among American wives have shown that there are a number of individual characteristics of women influencing the probability that they will be employed.

1. The greater the family economic need, the greater the probability of employment.[17] The relationship of employment status to family income (excluding wife's earnings) is monotonically declining and approximately linear. Other studies have shown that the overwhelming majority of working women give "economic" reasons for working.

2. The greater a woman's education, the higher her probability of employment.[18] Again the relationship is monotonic and nearly linear when the effects

---

[c]Because of a change in census procedure, the probability of having recent work experience is overstated, while the probability of returning tends to be understated in 1970.

of other confounding variables have been controlled. The usual interpretation of this relationship is that women with greater amounts of education are more likely to be able to obtain work if they want it, more likely to earn enough if they work to motivate them to seek work, and more likely to be motivated to seek work by virtue of their socialization into work roles and by virtue of the greater access to clean, light, and generally interesting employment opportunities.

3. Married women with children are more likely to work, the older their youngest child, and the fewer the number of children.[19]

4. Black wives are considerably more likely to be employed than white wives.[20]

5. Labor force participation varies with age, with peaks at around ages 20-24 and 45-54, and a trough in between. Net of the differential family status composition, age does not seem to exert a significant effect on employment, except that very young wives (under age twenty) have markedly lower employment rates than wives in their twenties and thirties and the employment of wives over the age of forty or forty-five declines with age.[21]

6. Studies of the employment of urban wives have found that employment rates are higher in those areas with an industrial structure and a heavy concentration of "female" jobs such as clerical occupations, light factory work, and service occupations. Employment rates are also higher in areas where female earnings (median earnings of full-year female workers) are relatively high.[22]

Changing Employment by Education

Employment rates have tended to increase for women at all education levels and at virtually all ages as shown in Table 3-7. Larger than average increases are found for women, age 25-34 with a college education—both women who completed 1-3 years of college and those who completed college. Both these groups had a 20-point increase between 1959 and 1973 in their employment rate in comparison to a 13-point increase for high-school graduates and a 7-point increase for high-school dropouts. Women, age 35-44, showed about a 10-point increase in the high-school-graduate, college-dropout, and college-graduate categories. Among younger women, age 20-24, there was a 10-point increase for both high-school dropouts and high-school graduates and for women with 1-3 years of college, and about a 16-point increase in the employment rate of college graduates. Among 20-24-year-old women in 1973, 86 percent of the college graduates were in the labor force in comparison to 71 percent, fourteen years earlier. At the older ages, there was relatively little increase in employment for women at any education category and in some categories there was a slight drop in the rate of employment.

Table 3-8 shows the rates of employment for mothers of children under the

Table 3-7
Changes in Labor Force Participation Rates for Women, by Education and Age:
1959 and 1973

	1959	1973	Change	Percent Change
20-24				
High school:				
1-3	31.5	42.0	10.5	33.3
4	51.0	62.9	11.9	23.3
College:				
1-3	47.4	58.7	11.3	23.8
4+	70.7	86.4	15.7	22.2
25-34				
High school:				
1-3	34.4	41.8	7.4	21.5
4	35.7	49.3	13.6	38.1
College:				
1-3	32.9	53.0	20.1	61.1
4+	44.7	64.0	19.3	43.2
35-44				
High school:				
1-3	45.3	52.9	7.6	16.8
4	42.9	55.5	12.6	29.4
College:				
1-3	41.4	53.1	11.7	28.3
4+	53.1	62.5	9.4	17.7
45-54				
High school:				
1-3	46.6	47.2	0.6	1.3
4	52.7	57.3	4.6	8.7
College:				
1-3	53.2	56.1	2.9	5.5
4+	69.4	63.5	−5.9	−8.5
55-64				
High school:				
1-3	35.7	39.8	4.1	10.3
4	41.4	47.1	5.7	13.8
College:				
1-3	45.7	48.1	2.4	5.3
4+	57.2	58.7	−1.5	−2.6

Table 3-7 (cont.)

Source: For 1973: U.S. Bureau of Labor Statistics, Special Labor Force Report #164, "Marital and Family Characteristics of the Labor Force, March 1973" (Washington, D.C.: U.S. Government Printing Office, 1974). For 1959: U.S. Bureau of Labor Statistics, Special Labor Force Report #2, "Marital and Family Characteristics of Workers: 1959" (Washington, D.C.: U.S. Government Printing Office, 1960).

Table 3-8

Employment Rates of Nonfarm Mothers of Young Children, by Education of Mother: 1970

Education	Age of Youngest Child		
	< 1 year	1 year	2 years
< 9 years	15.6	19.0	21.7
9-11	15.8	20.6	24.7
12	18.1	23.5	26.3
13-15	21.3	26.1	31.1
16+	20.2	27.6	34.5

Source: James A. Sweet and Vivien Lowe, "Returning to Work after Childbirth," CDE Working Paper 74-17, Center for Demography and Ecology, University of Wisconsin-Madison, 1974. Reprinted with permission of the Center for Demography and Ecology, University of Wisconsin.

age of three, by single year of age of the child enabling us to get an idea of the degree to which women are working shortly after the birth of their children. At all three ages of the youngest child, employment rates increase with increasing education. For women with children under age one, 16 percent of the women with 9-11 years of schooling were employed as compared to 20 percent of the women who were college graduates. For women with youngest child, age one, the differential is larger, with 21 percent of the high-school dropouts and 28 percent of the college graduates employed, while for women with youngest child age two, 25 percent of the high-school dropouts and 34 percent of the college graduates were employed at the time of the census.

Occupational Composition

Table 3-9 shows the occupational composition of married women in the period from 1960 to 1973 using data from the Current Population Survey. The occupational composition of the married female labor force has remained quite stable over the past decade and a half. The proportion of married women who

Table 3-9
Occupation Distribution of Married Women: 1960 and 1973

Occupation Group	1960	1973
Professional, technical, and kindred workers	12.9	16.1
Medical and other health workers	3.3	4.1
Teachers, except college	6.3	7.8
Other professional, technical, and kindred workers	3.3	4.2
Managers and administrators, except farm	5.0	5.2
Salaried workers	2.5	3.9
Self-employed workers	2.5	1.3
Sales workers	8.4	7.2
Clerical and kindred workers	28.3	34.0
Stenographers, typists, and secretaries	9.3	12.3
Other clerical and kindred workers	19.0	21.8
Craft and kindred workers	1.0	1.5
Operatives	18.6	15.1
Manufacturing	15.0	12.6
Other industries & transport equipment operatives	3.6	2.5
Laborers, except farm	.3	.7
Private household workers	6.2	2.6
Service workers, except private household	15.9	16.0
Food service workers	6.2	6.0
Other service workers	9.7	10.0
Farmers and farm managers	.2	.3
Farm laborers and supervisors	3.1	1.3

Source: U.S. Bureau of Labor Statistics, Special Labor Force Report #13, "Characteristics of Workers, March 1960" (Washington, D.C.: U.S. Government Printing Office, 1900); U.S. Bureau of Labor Statistics, Special Labor Force Report #164, "Marital and Family Characteristics of the Labor Force, March 1973" (Washington, D.C.: U.S. Government Printing Office, 1900).

are in clerical occupations has risen from around 28 percent to 34 percent. There was an increase from 6.3 to 7.8 percent in the proportion of married women who were teachers and also an increase from 3.3 to 4.1 percent in the proportion of women who are medical and health workers. The overall increase in the proportion of married women who were professionals was from 12.9 percent in 1960 to 16.1 percent in 1973. The proportion of women who were operatives declined from 18.6 to 15.1 percent. Private household workers also declined from 6.2 to 2.6 percent. There was virtually no change in the proportion of women who were service workers, sales workers, craft workers, or farmers. There was a continued drop in the proportion of women who were farm laborers such that by 1973 only 1.3 percent of all married women were in this occupation.

Has there been any significant change in the degree to which occupations are segregated by sex? Table 3-10 shows the proportion of persons in a number of specific occupations who are women. The similarities in these proportions between 1960 and 1970 are quite striking, but there are also a number of notable changes. In the major occupation groups the biggest change was in the proportion of women in clerical occupations which rose from 68 to 74 percent. There was a decline in proportion among female computer specialists, an occupation that grew in total size from 12,000 to 254,000 persons between 1960 and 1970.

Earnings of Women

Table 3-11 shows the median annual income for both men and women. At every age the median income more than doubled between 1959 and 1969. During this same period, the consumer price index increased by about 26 percent. At each age, with the exception of 20-24, the proportional increase in median earnings was greater for men than for women.

In considering the change in average annual earnings of women, we must be clear that there are several components of annual earnings including the hourly earnings of women, the number of hours worked per week, and the number of weeks worked per year. In a later section we will examine change in the week and hour components.

Annual earnings increase substantially with increases in education. Table 3-12 shows that the increase in annual earnings occurred at approximately the same rate for women at all education levels and ages. These are percentage increases and since the women with more education had a higher level of earnings to begin with, the absolute amount of their increase was larger than the increase for women with less education. The rate of increase for nonwhite women was considerably larger than the rate for white women. This is true at every education and age shown in the lower panel of the table.

Wives' Earnings as a Component
of Family Income

Table 3-13 shows two measures of the proportional contribution of wives' earnings to the family income. Between 1963 and 1973, the proportion of husband-wife families in which the wife had earnings increased from 59 to 69

Table 3-10
Proportion Female in Selected Occupations: 1960 and 1970

	% Female		% Change in Number of Female Workers
	1960	1970	
Professional, Technical & Kindred Workers	38.4	39.8	60.8
Accountants	16.4	26.0	127.8
Computer Specialists	29.8	19.6	1282.0
Engineers	.8	1.6	178.5
Lawyers & Judges	3.4	4.8	77.5
Life & Physical Scientists	8.3	13.1	105.9
Personnel & Labor Relations	32.9	30.7	166.6
Physicians, Dentists, Related Practices	5.9	8.5	66.7
Registered Nurses, Dieticians, Therapists	96.0	94.4	38.8
Health Technologists & Technicians	68.2	69.6	109.6
Religious Workers	16.5	10.3	−39.3
Social, Recreation Workers	60.0	58.6	115.7
Teachers, College & University	23.7	28.4	201.5
Teachers, except College & University	72.6	70.2	49.2
Elementary	85.8	83.6	40.2
Secondary	49.3	49.1	76.9
Engineering & Scientific Technicians	9.0	10.9	64.1
Writers, Artists, Entertainers	28.5	30.2	57.9
Managers & Administrators	14.7	16.5	22.3
Sales Workers	35.6	38.0	21.1
Insurance Agents, Brokers, Underwriters	9.6	12.4	60.3
Real Estate Agents & Brokers	23.9	31.9	81.4
Sales Persons & Clerks, N.E.C.	40.0	41.9	13.7
Sales Representatives: Manufacturing	10.4	8.4	−28.0
Sales Representatives: Wholesale	4.1	6.4	102.4
Sales Clerks: Retail	63.3	64.6	11.5
Sales Persons: Retail	10.7	12.9	22.3
Sales Persons of Services	22.1	33.5	72.0
Clerical & Kindred	68.0	73.5	54.5
Bank Tellers	70.1	86.2	130.7
Bookkeepers	83.4	82.0	62.7
Cashiers	76.9	83.5	85.9
Counter Clerks, except Food	61.0	66.6	105.9
Receptionists	93.0	94.7	97.9
Secretaries	97.1	97.6	85.4
Shipping & Receiving Clerks	8.0	14.5	142.2

Table 3-10 (cont.)

	% Female		% Change in Number of Female Workers
	1960	1970	
Stenographers	95.7	93.7	−53.6
Stock Clerks & Storekeepers	15.2	22.7	85.3
Telephone Operators	95.8	94.4	12.7
Typists	95.1	94.2	85.8
Crafts & Kindred Workers	3.1	5.0	78.6
Operatives, Except Transport	35.5	37.9	18.6
Transport Equipment Operatives	1.5	4.4	221.8
Bus Drivers	10.1	28.0	260.4
Delivery & Route Workers	3.2	3.2	41.6
Truck Drivers	−	1.5	−
Laborers Except Farm	5.2	8.4	55.5
Farmers & Farm Managers	4.7	4.6	−47.5
Farm Laborers & Farm Supervisors	16.7	15.2	−43.2
Service Workers Except Private Household	51.5	54.9	49.3
Cleaning Service Workers	32.6	31.7	40.7
Food Service Workers	67.6	68.0	34.9
Health Service Workers	83.1	88.2	77.9
Personal Service Workers	53.1	66.4	61.4
Protective Service Workers	3.7	6.1	124.7
Private Household Workers	96.4	96.6	−36.5
All Employed Persons	32.8	37.7	37.8

Source: C.B. Dicesare, "Changes in the Occupational Structure of U.S. Jobs," *Monthly Labor Review* (March 1975), pp. 24-34.

percent. In addition, among couples in which the wife had earnings, the proportional contribution to the family income also increased. In 1963, the median proportion of the family income contributed by wives (for couples in which the wife had income) was 21.1 percent. This median proportion rose to 26.7 percent in 1973. In 1963, 21.7 percent of the couples had wives' contributions to the family income of 40 percent or more. In 1973, this proportion had risen to 25.4 percent. The increase in the median proportion is found for both the white and nonwhite populations. The rise in employment of the rural farm population has been quite dramatic during this period.[23] The proportional contribution of wives to the family income was relatively constant

Table 3-11
Median Annual Income by Age (Persons with Income)

	Females			Males		
	1969[a]	1959	1969 ÷ 1959	1969[a]	1959	1969 ÷ 1959
20-24	$2696	$1251	2.16	$3653	$1701	2.14
25-34	3296	1308	2.52	7996	2734	2.92
35-44	3374	1364	2.47	9064	3085	2.93
45-54	3623	1332	2.72	8758	2979	2.94
	1969	1959	1969 ÷ 1959			
Consumer Price Index	109.8	87.3	1.26			

[a]Estimated from more detailed ages in source.

Sources: For 1969: U.S. Bureau of the Census, "1970 U.S. Census of Population, Detailed Characteristics," *U.S. Summary* PC(1)-D1 (Washington, D.C.: U.S. Government Printing Office), table 245; For 1959: U.S. Bureau of the Census of Population, Detailed Characteristics, *U.S. Summary* PC(1)-D1 (Washington, D.C.: U.S. Government Printing Office), table 219; U.S. Bureau of Labor Statistics, Consumer Price Index, *Handbook of Labor Statistics: 1973* (Washington, D.C.: U.S. Government Printing Office, 1974), table 121.

Table 3-12
Percentage Change in Female Median Earnings, by Age and Education: 1959-1969

		22-24	25-29	30-34	35-44	45-54
Total						
Education						
High School	1-3	72	69	67	65	55
	4	59	59	52	52	54
College	1-3	53	75	62	47	53
	4	49	73	64	60	55
	5+	43	66	66	68	66
Nonwhite						
Education						
High School	1-3	121	130	111	100	103
	4	142	117	95	87	100
College	1-3	123	105	96	87	96
	4	77	90	91	90	85
	5+	56	84	86	82	88

Source: U.S. Bureau of the Census, "U.S. Census of Population: 1970, Subject Reports, Educational Attainment," Final Report PC(2)-5B (Washington, D.C.: U.S. Government Printing Office, 1973), table 8; U.S. Bureau of the Census, "U.S. Census of Population: 1960, Subject Reports, Educational Attainment," Final Report PC(2)-5B (Washington, D.C.: U.S. Government Printing Office, 1963), table 7.

Table 3-13

Wife's Earnings as a Component of Family Income, for Married Couples in Which Wife Had Earnings: March 1963 and March 1973

	Median Proportion of Family Income		Percent of Couples in Which Wife's Earnings Contribute 40 Percent or More of Family Income	
	1963	1973	1963	1973
Age of Head				
<25	24.3	30.1	28.8	31.6
25+	20.9	26.3	21.2	24.7
Residence and Race				
Nonfarm	22.8	26.7	22.5	25.3
White	22.8	26.1	22.4	24.3
Nonwhite	23.0	31.8	22.8	33.9
Farm	4.1	26.4	14.4	27.4
Work Experience of Wife				
50-52, Full Time	37.4	38.1	43.7	35.2
27-49, Full Time	30.3	29.0	27.9	22.6
< 27 Weeks FT, or 1-52 PT	6.9	12.0	4.2	4.9
Family Income				
< $2000		19.2		33.0
$2000-2999		21.7		32.0
$3000-4999		22.7		30.1
$5000-6999		24.5		32.7
$7000-9999		25.4		29.4
$10,000-14,999		26.5		25.0
$15,000+		27.7		22.1
Total	21.1	26.7	21.7	25.4

Source: U.S. Bureau of Labor Statistics, Special Labor Force Report #164, "Marital and Family Characteristics of the Labor Force, 1973" (Washington, D.C.: U.S. Government Printing Office, 1974); U.S. Bureau of Labor Statistics, Special Labor Force Report #40, "Marital and Family Characteristics of Workers, 1963" (Washington, D.C.: U.S. Government Printing Office, 1964).

for couples in which the wife was usually a full-time worker during the previous year and in which she worked 27 or more weeks. There was a very large increase in the median proportion of the family income contributed by wives who worked less than 27 weeks full-time or who were usually working part-time. At all family income levels by 1973, the median proportion contributed by the wife is about the same. In general, the wives of younger men make a larger proportional contribution to family income than do the wives of older men as shown in Tables 3-13 and 3-14.

Table 3-14

Earnings of Wife as Percent of Family Income for Husband-Wife Families in Which Both Husband and Wife Had Earnings, by Race and Age of Husband: 1973

	White	Nonwhite
Total	24.6	31.0
Under 35 years	27.0	32.9
35 to 44 years	22.2	30.2
45 to 54 years	23.1	30.1
55 to 64 years	26.0	27.9
65 years and over	25.4	_[a]

[a]Base less than 75,000.

Source: U.S. Bureau of the Census, Current Population Reports, "Money Income in 1973 of Families and Persons in the United States," Series P-60, No. 97 (Washington, D.C.: U.S. Government Printing Office, 1975).

Changing Weeks and Hours Worked

In Table 3-15, between 1958 and 1971, there was a slight increase in the proportion of working women who usually worked full-time from 66.4 percent to 68.6 percent of the workers. There was, however, a major shift among the women who normally worked full-time toward a larger proportion working a full year. In 1958, 33 percent of all women with work experience worked full-time and a full year, whereas by 1971, 42 percent worked full-time and a full year. Among mothers of children, age 6-17, the increase in this proportion was quite similar to the total (33 to 41 percent), while among mothers with the youngest child, age 3-5, the proportion of full-time, full-year workers rose from 24 to 34 percent.

Employment Trends for Black Women

Among the largest and most pervasive differential in employment of women, particularly married women, is the one between black and white women. The employment rates of black women, particularly black women with young children, have been consistently higher than those for comparable white women for at least several decades. There has been a trend toward increasing employment of all women over the past fifteen years or so. Table 3-16 presents labor force participation rates for currently married nonwhite and white women by

Table 3-15

Distribution of Women with Work Experience, by Weeks Worked and Usual Hours Worked per Week: 1958-1971

	1958		1971	
Total				
Usually Worked				
Full Time				
Worked 50-52 Weeks	33.0		42.5	
27-49 Weeks	16.0	66.4	12.8	68.6
< 27 Weeks	17.4		33.3	
Part Time				
Worked 27-52 Weeks	19.1	33.5	18.9	31.3
< 27 Weeks	14.4		12.4	
Total	100.0		100.0	
Women with Youngest Child 6-17				
Usually Worked				
Full Time				
Worked 50-52 Weeks	33.2		41.2	
27-49 Weeks	15.4	63.1	11.9	63.8
< 27 Weeks	14.5		10.7	
Part Time				
Worked 27-52 Weeks	21.0	37.0	23.4	36.1
< 27 Weeks	16.0		12.7	
Total	100.0		100.0	
Women with Youngest Child 3-5				
Usually Worked				
Full Time				
Worked 50-52 Weeks	24.1		34.1	
27-49 Weeks	13.6	60.1	11.8	61.3
< 27 Weeks	22.4		15.4	
Part Time				
Worked 27-52 Weeks	21.7	40.0	21.6	38.8
< 27 Weeks	18.3		17.2	
Total	100.0		100.0	

Source: For 1958: U.S. Bureau of Labor Statistics, Special Labor Force Report #2, "Marital and Family Characteristics of Workers, 1959" (Washington, D.C.: U.S. Government Printing Office, 1960), table H; For 1971: U.S. Bureau of Labor Statistics, Special Labor Force Report #153, "Marital and Family Characteristics of Workers, 1972" (Washington, D.C.: U.S. Government Printing Office, 1973), table M.

Table 3-16

Labor Force Participation Rates for White and Nonwhite Married Women, by Family Status: March 1973

	Black and Other Races	White	Nonwhite Rate as Percent of White Rate
No children < 18	49.1	42.7	1.15
Age 16-34	65.4	75.1	.87
Age 35+	44.6	34.7	1.28
Children 6-17	60.5	47.8	1.27
Age 16-34	69.7	53.1	1.46
Age 35+	59.0	48.1	1.23
Children 3-5, None < 3	57.3	34.6	1.66
Children < 3	48.5	25.5	1.90

Source: U.S. Bureau of Labor Statistics, Special Labor Force Report #164, "Marital and Family Characteristics of the Labor Force, March 1973" (Washington, D.C.: U.S. Government Printing Office, 1974), tables F and I.

family status. The nonwhite rate for women with children under the age of three is 48.5 percent in comparison to a rate of 25.5 percent for white women. Thus, the nonwhite rate is 90 percent higher than the white rate. The differential is somewhat smaller, 66 percent for women with the youngest child, age 3-5. For women with older children, the differentials are even smaller. Those nonwhite women with children, age 6-17, who are themselves 35 years or older have employment rates that are 23 percent higher than those of white women. The only exception to the white-nonwhite differential in employment rates is for young recently married nonwhite women with no children under age 18 who have a rate somewhat lower than that of comparable white women. Young unmarried black women tend to have rates that are lower than those for white women. In our earlier analysis, we were able to show that the white-nonwhite differential in employment is not due to differences in education of the women, nor to differences in family economic need. The nonwhite (and presumably the black) rate is higher for every education level and every economic need level.

There are two important differentials in the pattern of employment between blacks and whites that should be noted. The first is that for white women, the rate of employment declines rather sharply with increases in the husband's income. For nonwhite women this is not the case. Wives of men earning $10,000 or $15,000 per year are no less likely to be working than are wives of men earning $3,000 or $4,000 per year. Similarly, white women show a monotonic increase in employment rates with increases in education. For black women this is not the case. There is very little difference in the employment rates by education except that college-graduate black women have much higher rates than those with less education and the differential in the employment rates between blacks and whites is much larger for college-educated women than for women with less education.[24]

Black-White Differences in Earnings of Married Women

Overall the annual earnings of black women are only about three-fifths those of white women. This is due to some extent to the heavier concentration of black women in the lower education categories where earnings for both races tend to be much much lower. However, there is a substantial annual earnings differential between blacks and whites at every level of education. In 1959, for example, black women who were high-school dropouts or high-school graduates earned about 70 percent of the amount earned by white women with the same education level. The black-white differential is larger for women who have less than a high-school education (about 55 percent), but for women who are college graduates there is virtually no earnings differential at all.[25]

Changing Occupational Distributions

There were some important shifts in the occupational distribution for black women between 1960 and 1973. Table 3-17 shows the occupational distribution for nonwhite women separately for women under the age of 35 and for women 35 and over. For both groups there was a marked rise in the proportion of women in the white-collar occupations, a slight rise in the proportion in operative occupations, a dramatic decline in the proportion who were private household workers, and a decline in the proportion who were farm workers. For the younger group, there was a decline in the service occupations other than private household work, while for the older women there was a continued increase in this occupation. The most dramatic shift in this table is the one out of private household occupations and into the clerical occupations. Nearly 29 percent of nonwhite women under age 35 were in private household work in 1960, while by 1973 there were only about 6 percent. Clerical workers accounted for 14 percent of the nonwhite women under age 35 in 1960, and 35.5 percent in 1973. By 1973, the proportion of nonwhite women under age 35 in clerical occupations was nearly as high for nonwhites as for whites (35.5 percent vs. 39 percent), although for women, age 35 and over, there remains a very large differential in the proportion of clerical workers—32.5 percent for white vs. 15.0 percent for nonwhite women.

Table 3-17

Occupation Distribution of Employed Women, for Nonwhite Women, Age 14-34 and 35 and Over: 1960 and 1973

	14-34[a]		35 and over	
	1960	1973	1960	1973
Professional, Technical, etc.	9.7	13.5	7.2	11.6
Managers and Administrative	0.7	2.6	1.6	2.9
Clerical	14.3	35.5	5.9	15.0
Sales	2.2	2.9	1.7	2.0
Craft	0.7	0.8	0.8	1.2
Operatives	14.9	16.9	13.3	14.5
Private Household Workers	28.8	6.0	42.9	20.9
Service, except Private Household	23.5	20.3	21.9	29.8
Farm	4.1	0.6	3.7	1.0
Laborers	1.1	0.9	1.0	1.1
Total	100.0	100.0	100.0	100.0

[a]16-34 in 1970.

Source: For 1960: U.S. Bureau of Labor Statistics, Special Labor Force Report #7, "Marital and Family Characteristics of Workers, 1960" (Washington, D.C.: U.S. Government Printing Office, 1960); For 1973: U.S. Bureau of Labor Statistics, Special Labor Force Report #164, "Marital and Family Characteristics of the Labor Force, 1973" (Washington, D.C.: U.S. Government Printing Office, 1974).

Table 3-18 shows some measures of occupational sorting for women with specific amounts of education, for both 1960 and 1970, and for the total female population as well as for the nonwhite population. The first panel shows the proportion of women who were high-school graduates and did not continue with any additional education who are employed in operative, service, and laborer occupations. We see that about one-quarter of all women and over half of the nonwhite women, with a high school diploma, are employed in these blue-collar occupations as of 1970. This proportion declined for nonwhite women (associated probably with the decline in the prevalence of private household work), but increased slightly for the total population. There remains, as of 1970, a substantially larger proportion of nonwhite high-school graduates in blue-collar occupations.

The bottom two panels of the table show the percent of women employed in professional and managerial occupations among women who completed 13-15 years of education and among women who completed 16 or more years of education. Among college dropouts, nonwhites have lower than average proportions in the professional and managerial occupations in both 1960 and 1970 but the differential has been to contract between the two census years. There is a

Table 3-18

Selected Occupational Measure for Selected Age and Education Groups of Females, by Race: 1960-1970

	1970		1960	
	Total	Nonwhite	Total	Nonwhite
Percent Employed in Operative, Service, and Laborer Occupations				
Education—12 years				
25+ older	28.2	55.0	25.5	59.6
22-24	28.8	45.5	22.6	57.9
25-29	31.4	51.1	25.4	59.8
30-34	30.3	52.7	26.6	58.2
35-44	28.5	55.4	26.9	58.0
45-54	26.5	57.5	23.4	63.1
Percent Employed in Professional and Managerial Occupations				
Education—13-15 years				
25+ older	33.7	27.3	36.5	22.8
22-24	24.6	18.0	35.2	16.5
25-29	30.0	21.6	36.5	22.4
30-34	34.4	26.0	34.1	20.9
35-44	34.0	29.8	31.4	19.8
45-54	32.5	29.5	38.8	26.5
Percent Employed in Professional and Managerial Occupations				
Education—16 years				
25+ older	78.2	83.3	73.7	75.3
22-24	78.6	77.9	77.7	77.9
25-29	81.9	84.5	76.9	76.5
30-34	81.6	85.5	72.1	74.5
35-44	78.5	84.6	71.9	75.7
45-54	74.3	78.9	74.9	75.9

Sources: For 1970: U.S. Bureau of the Census, "U.S. Census of Population: 1970, Subject Reports, Educational Attainment," Final Report PC(2)-5B (Washington, D.C.: U.S. Government Printing Office, 1970), table 11; For 1960: U.S. Bureau of the Census, U.S. Census of Population: 1960, Subject Reports, Educational Attainment," Final Report PC(2)-5B (Washington, D.C.: U.S. Government Printing Office, 1960), table 8.

tendency for a lower proportion of college dropouts to be in professional and managerial occupations in 1970 than in 1960. For women who graduated from college, nonwhite women have a higher-than-average prevalence of professional and managerial occupations; and for both the total and the nonwhite population, there was a tendency for the proportion in professional and managerial occupations to increase during this decade.

Attitudes Toward Working Women

Another area of considerable interest, about which rather little is known, is the nature of attitudes toward employment of women, particularly toward the employment of the mothers of young children in the United States. In their 1965 study, Morgan et al. asked a sample of husbands a question:[26] "Suppose a family has children but they are all in school. Would you say it is a good thing for the wife to take a job or bad thing or what?" The responses were distributed:

15 percent had entirely favorable attitudes,
17 percent had favorable attitudes with qualifications,
17 percent had "pro/con" or "depends" attitudes,
14 percent had unfavorable attitudes with qualifications, and
35 percent had unfavorable attitudes.

More favorable attitudes tended to be characteristic of nonwhite husbands and of husbands who were younger than average. An earlier study conducted in 1960 by Morgan et al. asked a similar question:[27] "There are many wives who have jobs these days. Do you think it is a good thing for a wife to work or a bad thing or what?" In that study the responses of family heads (predominantly males) were distributed:

 9 percent had favorable attitudes,
14 percent had favorable attitudes with qualifications,
16 percent had "pro/con" or "depends" attitudes,
10 percent had unfavorable attitudes with qualifications, and
18 percent had unfavorable attitudes.

That question included no reference to children.

More recently, the 1970 National Fertility Study asked a series of questions on sex role attitudes of married women in the reproductive ages. A listing of these questions and summary of the responses to them is presented in Table 3-19. Mason and Bumpass have analyzed these data and report:

The most impressive finding . . . is the continuing strong support for the segregation of basic roles by sex. Over three-quarters of U.S. women agree that it is better for everyone if the man is the achiever while the woman is the homemaker and mother. . . . Responses to the other two items suggests that the strong consensus on the first refers to men's and women's basic responsibilities rather than to a total segregation of their activities. Although most women think it best when women are responsible for the home, close to half of them believe that women have a right to a career. . . . Similarly, a rather surprising one-half of whites and close to three-quarters of the blacks feel that men are obligated to share household chores with wives. . . . Support for the much discussed principle of equal pay for equal work is close to unanimous in the 1970 sample, regardless of women's ages or their race.[28]

Table 3-19

Attitudes Toward Traditional Sex-Based Division of Labor, Employment Rights of Women, Work and Maternal Role, and Sex-Difference Stereotypes and Socialization, by Age (Percent Agreeing with Items)

Attitude Item	Total	<30	30+
a) It is much better for everyone involved if the man is the achiever outside the home and the woman takes care of the home and family.	78	76	79
b) A woman should not let bearing and rearing children stand in the way of a career if she wants it.	49	50	49
c) Men should share the work around the house with women such as doing dishes, cleaning, and so forth.	53	53	53
d) Men and women should be paid the same money if they do the same work.	95	96	94
e) On the job, men should not refuse to work under women.	72	73	71
f) A woman should have exactly the same job opportunities as a man.	63	65	62
g) Women should be considered as seriously as men for jobs as executives, politicians, or even President.	55	57	54
h) There should be free child-care centers so that women could take jobs.	45	48	43
i) A woman's job should be kept for her when she is having a baby.	58	61	56
j) If anything happened to one of the children while the mother was working, she could never forgive herself.	45	45	45
k) A working mother can establish just as warm and secure a relationship with her children as a mother who does not work.	47	47	46
l) A pre-school child is likely to suffer if his mother works.	71	69	72
m) Women are happier if they stay at home and take care of their children.	41	40	41
n) A man can make long range plans for his life, but a woman has to take things as they come.	31	30	31
o) Sex seems to exist mainly for the man's pleasure.	18	16	19
p) Many of those in women's rights organizations today seem to be unhappy misfits.	53	51	56
q) Young girls are entitled to as much independence as young boys.	47	49	46
Number of Cases	6740	3098	3642

Source: K.O. Mason and L.L. Bumpass, "Women's Sex-Role Attitudes in the United States, 1970." CDE Working Paper 73-27, Center for Demography & Ecology, University of Wisconsin-Madison, 1973, tables 1-4. Reprinted with permission of the Center for Demography and Ecology, University of Wisconsin.

They also note:

That working women should feel particularly guilty if something happened to their children is supported by less than half the population. . . . And about the same proportion endorses the idea that a working mother's relationship with children can be just as warm and psychologically secure as a nonworking one's. . . . It is with regard to a mother's relation to her *preschool* children, then, that attitudes remain highly traditional. . . . Here, close to three-quarters of whites . . . feel that preschool children indeed suffer if a mother works. This belief may be a key attitude in contemporary sex-role ideology, not only because it is likely to promote a gap between women's status and men's by encouraging women to periodically drop out of the labor force, but also because it may underlie the continued support for the generalized division of labor. So long as most women feel that their absence from the home or commitment to work harms their preschool children, most are also likely to feel that the traditional gender division between homemaking and achievement is best.[29]

Mason has been concerned with attempting to measure recent change in sex role attitudes.[30] There have been no good replications of similar questions asked of similar samples in the United States from which it is possible to measure change. Mason[31] and Mason, Czajka, and Arber[32] have attempted to compare sex role attitudes measured in the 1970 National Fertility Study with those measured in a 1973 survey conducted in North Carolina by means of a matching procedure. They find in the 1973 North Carolina study considerably higher levels of egalitarian sex role attitudes and also a tendency for the various sex role attitudes to be more highly correlated among themselves, suggesting a greater consistency of attitudes on various aspects of sex role equality.

Effects of Mothers Working

There is relatively little research on the actual effects of mothers working on infants and preschool children. In a recent review article Etaugh notes the absence of research, particularly on effects on preschool children, and, in general, concludes that research to date shows little, if any adverse effect of maternal employment on children.[33] Whatever the actual effects may be, mothers of young children are exposed to a culture that discourages their employment, although these cultural messages, at least in the mass media, may be fewer and less intensive than they were a decade ago. There remains a very strong set of negative attitudes toward maternal employment for mothers of young children.

Conclusion

In summary, we have noted major shifts in the levels of employment and in the patterns of employment through the life cycle. More women, particularly those with young children, are working every year. Marriage and reproductive patterns have recently shifted toward later marriages, smaller families, and later beginning of childbearing. American women are increasingly continuing their education beyond high school.

All of these recent trends seem to be conditions necessary to increased equality of opportunity in the labor market. It will be important to monitor the sex differences in occupation composition and earnings, particularly for younger women, over the next decade or so. Up to this time there has been little, if any, improvement in the relative status of American women in these areas.

Notes

1. For excellent discussions of longer run trends in employment of women, see G. Bancroft, *The American Labor Force: Its Growth and Changing Composition* (New York: Wiley, 1958); I.B. Tauber and C. Tauber, *People of the United States in the 20th Century* (Washington, D.C.: U.S. Government Printing Office, 1971); V.K. Oppenheimer, *The Female Labor Force in the United States: Demographic and Economic Factors Governing the Growth and Changing Composition*, Population Monograph Series No. 5 (Berkeley: University of California Press, 1970); C. Long, *The Labor Force under Changing Income and Employment* (Princeton: Princeton University Press, 1958); J.D. Durand, *The Labor Force in the United States: 1890 to 1960* (New York: Social Science Research Council, 1948); R.W. Smuts, *Women and Work in America* (New York: Schocken, 1971); E.F. Baker, *Technology and Woman's Work* (New York: Columbia University Press, 1964); R.A. Easterlin, *Population, Labor Force, and Long Swings in Economic Growth*, National Bureau of Economic Research General Series, No. 86 (New York: Columbia University Press, 1968); W.G. Bowen and T.A. Finegan, *The Economics of Labor Force Participation* (Princeton: Princeton University Press, 1969).

2. Smuts, op. cit., p. 38.

3. Ibid., p. 51.

4. For discussion of recent fertility trends see L.A. Westoff and C.F. Westoff, *From Now to Zero: Fertility, Contraception and Abortion in America* (Boston: Little, Brown, 1971); N.B. Ryder and C.F. Westoff, *Reproduction in the United States: 1965* (Princeton: Princeton University Press, 1971); J.A. Sweet, "Differentials in the Rate of Fertility Decline: 1960-1970," *Family Planning Perspectives* 6, No. 2 (Spring, 1974), pp. 103-107; L.L. Bumpass, "Fertility Behavior of American Women," in W. Montagna and W.A. Sadler, eds., *Reproductive Behavior* (New York: Plenum, 1975), pp. 319-332; National Center for Health Statistics, "Natality Statistics Analysis: United States, 1965-1967," *Vital and Health Statistics*, Series 21, No. 19 (May, 1970); U.S. Bureau of the Census, "Fertility Indicators: 1970," *Current Population Reports*, Series P-23, No. 36 (Washington, D.C.: U.S. Government Printing Office, 1971);

U.S. Bureau of the Census, "Fertility Histories and Birth Expectations of American Women: June 1971," *Current Population Reports*, Series P-20, No. 263 (Washington, D.C.: U.S. Government Printing Office, 1974); U.S. Bureau of the Census, "Fertility Expectations of American Women: June 1974," *Current Population Reports*, Series P-20, No. 277 (Washington, D.C.: U.S. Government Printing Office, 1975).

5. U.S. Bureau of the Census, "Fertility Expectations of American Women," op. cit. For alternative interpretations see J. Blake, "Can We Believe Recent Data on Birth Expectations in the United States?" *Demography* 11, No. 1 (February, 1974), pp. 25-44; L.L. Bumpass, "Comment on J. Blake's 'Can We Believe Recent Data on Birth Expectations in the United States?' " *Demography* 12, No. 1 (February, 1975), pp. 155-156.

6. J. Sklar and B. Berkov, "Abortion, Illegitimacy, and the American Birth Rate," *Population Reprint Series*, No. 449, International Population and Urban Research, Institute of International Studies, University of California-Berkeley, 1974; E.F. Jones and C.F. Westoff, "Attitudes Toward Abortion in the United States in 1970 and the Trend since 1965," in Commission on Population Growth and the American Future, Research Reports, Vol. I, *Demographic and Social Aspects of Population Growth*, C.F. Westoff and R. Parke, Jr., eds. (Washington, D.C.: U.S. Government Printing Office, 1972).

7. R.R. Rindfuss and C.F. Westoff, "The Initiation of Contraception," *Demography* 11, No. 1 (February, 1974), pp. 75-87.

8. J. Berent, "Fertility and Family Planning in Europe around 1970: A Comparative Study of 12 National Surveys: Some Preliminary Findings," presented at the 1974 annual meetings of the Population Association of America.

9. L.L. Bumpass, "Fertility Differences by Employment Patterns and Role Attitudes," CDE Working Paper 74-23, Center for Demography and Ecology, University of Wisconsin-Madison, 1974.

10. R.A. Easterlin, "Population," in Neil W. Chamberlain, ed., *Contemporary Economic Issues* rev. ed. (Homewood, Illinois: Irwin, 1972); R.A. Easterlin, "Relative Economic Status and the American Fertility Swing," in Eleanor B. Sheldon, ed., *Family Economic Behavior: Problems and Prospects* (Philadelphia: Lippincott, 1973), pp. 170-223; R.A. Easterlin, "The Economics and Sociology of Fertility: A Synthesis," in Charles Tilly, ed., *Historical Studies of Changing Fertility* (Princeton: Princeton University Press, forthcoming).

11. J.A. Sweet, "Differentials in the Rate of Fertility Decline: 1960-1970," op. cit.

12. For discussions of marriage patterns, see H. Carter and P.C. Glick, *Marriage and Divorce: A Social and Economic Study* (Cambridge: Harvard University Press, 1970); P. Glick and A. Norton, "Perspectives on the Recent Upturn in Divorce and Remarriage," *Demography* 10, No. 3 (August, 1973), pp. 301-314; K. Davis, "The American Family in Relation to Demographic Change,"

in Commission on Population Growth and the American Future, Research Reports, Vol. I, *Demographic and Social Aspects of Population Growth*, C.F. Westoff and R. Parke, Jr., eds. (Washington, D.C.: U.S. Government Printing Office, 1972); National Center for Health Statistics, "Teenagers: Marriages, Divorces, Parenthood, and Mortality," *Vital and Health Statistics*, Series 21, No. 23 (August, 1973); National Center for Health Statistics, "Marriages: Trends and Characteristics, United States," *Vital and Health Statistics*, Series 21, No. 21 (September, 1971); A.L. Ferriss, *Indicators of Change in the American Family* (New York: Russell Sage Foundation, 1970); U.S. Bureau of the Census, "Social and Economic Variations in Marriage, Divorce, and Remarriage: 1967," *Current Population Reports*, Series P-20, No. 223, (Washington, D.C.: U.S. Government Printing Office, 1971).

13. For additional information on educational trends see A.L. Ferriss, *Indicators of Trends in American Education* (New York: Russell Sage Foundation, 1969); W.V. Grant and C.G. Lind, *Digest of Educational Statistics: 1973*, DHEW Publication (OE)-74-11103 (Washington, D.C.: U.S. Government Printing Office, 1974).

14. J.A. Sweet, "Employment During Pregnancy," CDE Working Paper 74-16, Center for Demography and Ecology, University of Wisconsin-Madison, 1974.

15. For a discussion of legal aspects of maternity benefits, see J.G. Gutwillig, "Job-related Maternity Benefits," remarks for the Kentucky Hospital Personnel Association, April 16-18, 1973; E.D. Koontz, "Childbirth and Child Rearing Leave: Job-related Benefits," *New York Law Forum* 17, No. 2 (1971).

16. J.A. Sweet and V. Lowe, "Return to Work after Childbirth," CDE Working Paper 74-17, Center for Demography and Ecology, University of Wisconsin-Madison, 1974.

17. W.G. Bowen and T.A. Finegan, op. cit., Chapter 5.

18. Ibid., p. 116.

19. J.A. Sweet, *Women in the Labor Force* (New York: Seminar Press, 1973).

20. Ibid.; W.G. Bowen and T.A. Finegan, op. cit., p. 90.

21. J.A. Sweet, *Women in the Labor Force*, op. cit., Chapter 4.

22. Bowen and Finegan, op. cit., Chapter 6; G. Cain, *Married Women in the Labor Force: An Economic Analysis* (Chicago: University of Chicago Press, 1966).

23. For a discussion of employment patterns of farm wives as of 1970, see J.A. Sweet, "Trends and Differentials in the Fertility of the Rural Farm Population," CDE Working Paper 74-12, Center for Demography and Ecology, University of Wisconsin-Madison, 1974.

24. Sweet, *Women in the Labor Force*, op. cit., Chapter 4.

25. Ibid., Chapter 7.

26. J. Morgan, I. Sirageldin, and N. Baerwaldt, "Productive Americans: A Study of How Individuals Contribute to Economic Growth" (Ann Arbor: Institute for Social Research, University of Michigan, 1966).

27. J. Morgan, M.H. David, W.J. Cohen, and H.E. Brazer, *Income and Welfare in the United States* (New York: McGraw-Hill, 1962).

28. K.O. Mason and L.L. Bumpass, "Women's Sex Role Attitudes in the United States, 1970," CDE Working Paper 73-27, Center for Demography and Ecology, University of Wisconsin-Madison, 1973. Reprinted with the permission of the Center for Demography and Ecology, University of Wisconsin, Madison, Wisconsin.

29. Ibid. Reprinted with the permission of the Center for Demography and Ecology, University of Wisconsin, Madison, Wisconsin.

30. K.O. Mason, "Studying Change in Sex Role Definitions via Attitude Data," Social Statistics Section, Proceedings of the American Statistical Association, 1973; K.O. Mason, "Women's Labor Force Participation and Fertility," Final Report 21U-662, prepared for NIH, DHEW, under Contract 71-2212 (with the assistance of B.S. Schulz), 1974.

31. Mason, "Studying Change in Sex Role Definitions via Attitude Data," op. cit.

32. K.O. Mason, J. Czajka, and S. Arber, "Recent Change in Women's Sex Role Attitudes," Draft (cited with the permissions of the authors), 1974.

33. C. Etaugh, "Effects of Maternal Employment on Children: A Review of Recent Research," *Merrill-Palmer Quarterly of Behavior and Development*, 20, No. 2 (1974). See also F.I. Nye and L.W. Hoffman, *The Employed Mother in America* (Chicago: Rand McNally, 1963); L.W. Hoffman and F.I. Nye, *Working Mothers: An Evaluative Review of the Consequences for Wife, Husband and Child* (San Francisco: Jossey-Bass, 1974).

4

Female Status: A New Population Policy

Virginia Gray

In a recent paper this author documented the ways in which women are both victims and beneficiaries of population policy in the United States.[1] The status of women in the eyes of the "population professions" is not high: demographic theory and research on the household does not adequately recognize the independence of the woman. Some female demographers are attempting to change this situation through their own research and by pressuring the National Institute of Health to put more women in important positions. Feminists also criticize the male bias of the medical profession, which both develops contraceptive technology and dispenses it. The principal objections are to the emphasis of research predominantly directed at female rather than male contraceptive devices and to the dangerous side effects of contraceptives too routinely prescribed for women.

In this chapter we are going to concentrate on a set of policies that achieve the societal goal of lowering population growth and my normative goal of benefitting women. These are status of women policies (hereinafter shortened to female status), policies that attempt to equalize the sexes and to give women independent rather than derived status. From this set we will focus on the right to vote as a past population policy and the Equal Rights Amendment as a future population policy.

First, some definitions are needed. *Population policy* is defined broadly as "government action (or inaction) toward objectives which involve the influencing of population characteristics."[2] *Population characteristics* are the size, growth, distribution, and composition of the population. *Female status policies* are thought to decrease the birth rate, which is a determinant of population growth (usually the concern of demographers), and to change the composition of the female population by increasing the income, education, and employment of women relative to that of men (usually a concern of feminists).

The Social Context of Reproductive Decisions

Now we turn to an examination of societal pressures in influencing individual reproductive decisions and governmental policies. Society provides cues that motivate women to have children (pronatalism) or to prevent births through

67

contraception or abortion (antinatalism). Both can be coercive or mandatory in nature so that women do not have the power of decision about motherhood. In particular, societal norms about reproduction and women's roles affect one's decision to employ contraception; societal pressures help determine the value placed on having children versus engaging in some other activity. At one extreme are the coercive pronatalist influences identified by Judith Blake: Freudian psychology, cross-cultural sociological studies showing the functionality of the female role, legal taboos against homosexuality, sexually specific personality traits, and childhood socialization.[3] To change from pronatalism would involve a change in individual and societal utilities. These changes are political in nature—they are not just a matter of providing better birth control technology. A more moderate position is the "voluntary" position of family planning, i.e., the belief that birth control allows each couple to choose how many children to have. However, family planning could be compatible with pronatalism; for instance, a woman could use the birth control pill to space the births of four children. "Voluntary" family planners tend to treat overpopulation as a disease to be solved by medical technology, and thus they overlook motivation, asserts Kingsley Davis.[4] Changes in motivation for childbirth would involve radical societal changes in the structure of the family, the status of women, and sexual mores.

The most extreme antinatalists advocate moving "beyond family planning" to mandatory fertility control, e.g., putting a fertility control agent in the water supply, issuing licenses for childbirth, or sterilization.[5] Somehow these permanent solutions always seem to be aimed at women, not men, and can be stated in innocuous ways intended to imply voluntary action: "The woman may choose to be sterilized or go to jail." "The woman may choose to be sterilized or lose her welfare benefits."

A more moderate antinatalist position is taken by feminists, who seek to lift the pressures to reproduce rather than to impose pressures not to reproduce. There are several indications that feminism is spreading antinatalism throughout women of all social classes. In April 1972, *Redbook* magazine did a survey of its readers and found that fewer than 2 percent of the 120,000 women who responded believe that "women can best develop their potential by being good wives and mothers."[6] A survey in late 1973 of blue-collar wives, 20-49 years old, in 8 metropolitan areas showed the most significant change in attitudes in the last 25 years, a movement toward the idea that women should be able to choose a career, marriage, or both.[7] Almost a third of the wives said they would not choose homemaking if they were 15 today; the younger women want two children or less, compared to an ideal family size of four in a 1965 survey.

The Relation of Fertility and
Compositional Variables

Within an environment of conflicting strains of pronatalism and antinatalism, the fertility rate first fell to 2.1 children, the net replacement level, and then in

1973 to 1.9 children, with all indications that the trend continued through 1974. One well-documented relationship, among the many possible causes, will be discussed here as it has held the interest of both demographers and feminists.

The Consistent Inverse Relationship
Between Female Employment and Fertility

Evidence

At the individual level there is a good deal of evidence, principally from the National Fertility Studies, establishing this relationship and also the positive association of employment, education, desired family size, and use of contraceptives, though the causal connections are not so well-established.[8] For example, employed women are twice as likely to be childless as are women not in the labor force.[9] This relationship is stronger for educated women with higher status jobs. Twenty percent of women in higher status occupations remain childless, while 10-15 percent of women in lower status jobs are childless. Female social scientists are one of the less-fertile groups. In 1960, over one-third of ever-married white women, age 35-44, in social science were childless and the whole group of female social scientists averaged only 1.35 children.

At the aggregate level the relationship is similar but more complex. Demographic studies, based on census data from countries in different stages of development, show that, historically, economic and social development, as well as the means to limit births, must be present before birth rates begin to fall sharply. More recent variations in development patterns have led some demographers to focus on the equality of the distribution of economic and social benefits within a country. These demographers suggest that motivation to limit births must come from new development strategies such as career alternatives to motherhood.[10] It has even been suggested that economic development may increase the level of fertility unless the economic and social benefits are distributed equally among men and women.[11]

Explanations

Let us turn to explanations of the association of employment (and similar variables) with fertility and consider their policy implications. There is a debate here over what is the cause and what is the effect. In turn, there is disagreement over whether affording women opportunities to learn and to work will increase or decrease the birth rate. One explanation is that of role incompatibility—it is the incompatibility between the roles of mother and worker that causes the fertility differential between workers and nonworkers.[12]

The policy implication is that establishing day care centers or having fathers participate in child care may free women from the drudgery that has kept them from having more children. One author (male) concludes, "What's good for women's lib may not be good for the nation."[13] Though statistics showing the high incidence of mental disturbance among women (relative to men) might be used to support the role strain explanation, I would conclude "what is good for the nation (in terms of reducing birth rates) is not good for women."[14]

Another common explanation is motivation. Education motivates women to practice contraception because the costs of children are higher for the educated who forfeit promising employment opportunities. In fact, there has been a calculation of how the cost to a woman of each successive child varies by education level.[15] The figure includes the direct costs (college education, hospital bills, food, and clothing) and the opportunity costs, i.e., what the mother could have earned had she worked outside the house for the first fourteen years of each child's life. The total direct and opportunity costs (discounted) for the first child born to a woman with elementary school education is $84,045; for a woman with five or more years of college the total cost is $142,947 for the first and $55,030 for each additional child.

The motivational effects of employment opportunities may work more effectively against the possibility of large families since many educated and employed women still desire one child. The President's Commission on Population Growth and the American Future examined the evidence on fertility and employment and concluded that policies facilitating the combining of the roles of mother and worker reduce fertility in the long run.[16]

There are doubtless many other explanations but these two offer a contrast in their policy implications for women. Policies of role incompatibility may achieve the societal goal of reducing population growth but do not achieve feminist goals. The motivational policies may achieve both goals as long as the motivation is not supplied through coercion. We will adopt the motivational explanation for the moment and argue that policies supplying motivation by improving the status of women are thus important indirect population policies. In demographic studies change in the roles or status of women is often mentioned though no one seems to have measured its impact systematically as will be attempted later in this chapter.[17]

Measures of Female Status

In fact, we have located only one study that attempts to develop a theory of female status and to measure its existence.[18] Sanday hypothesizes that female status (defined in terms of the number of economic and political rights which accrue to women) is a function of significant participation in subsistence or warfare activities. These are usually male spheres while reproduction is usually the female sphere. She develops a Guttman scale of four items (female control over produce, demand for female produce, female participation in political activities, and presence of female solidarity groups) with a coefficient of reproducibility of 0.92 and applies it cross-culturally. She finds female contribution to production to be a necessary but not sufficient condition for the development of female status; control and production must be linked in a competitive market if female labor is to lead to high female status. Since the use of contraceptives is so interrelated with the use of political and economic rights by women, let us consider two limiting cases: (1) where no women have access to effective modern contraceptives and (2) where all women have access to modern contraceptives. Assume that the latter situation characterizes the present where the birth rate is already low. Further advances in contraceptive technology will have little marginal effect unless motivation to contracept is increased. In this case policies improving the female status such as the Equal Rights Amendment might have a greater marginal effect.

The Effect of Female Status
in the Past

Now let us look at the first case: a situation where no women have access to modern contraceptive devices. Thus, a couple is left with celibacy, rhythm, diaphragm, douche, coitus interruptus, etc.—all less than 100 percent effective. If one could show that female status supplied enough motivation that fertility declined even when contraception is technologically backward, then one could argue with more support that female status would have a similar negative effect on the fertility rate when contraception is technologically advanced.

Now we must search about for a situation representative of the first case. We have selected for this purpose the period of the 1920s in this country when modern contraception was not yet available. As a measure of female status for this period we have selected the granting of suffrage to women by states. We assume the right to vote is a policy granting significant status to women and hypothesize that it in turn motivates them to decrease fertility. Since 12 states implemented this policy before the adoption of the 19th Amendment in 1920, we have a natural field experiment without premeasurement. The 12 states granting suffrage between 1892 and 1916 constitute the experimental group (Wyoming, Colorado, Utah, Idaho, Washington, California, Kansas, Oregon, Arizona, Montana, Nevada, and Illinois) while the remaining states constitute the control group.

We wish to determine if the birth rate is significantly lower in the experimental group than in the control group; if so, we will attribute that difference to the enactment of suffrage. Since other variables may be affecting the birth rate and female status, we also do regression analysis with female employment, illiteracy, and presence of suffrage included as independent variables.

Comparison of Means. The first exercise is to compare birth rate means between the two groups. We use two birth rate measures: the crude birth rate averaged for stability over a three year period [crude birth rate = (# births)/(# women) × 1000] and the general fertility rate [general fertility rate = (# births to women age 15-44)/(# women age 15-44) × 1000] in 1920.[a] The three year average for each state begins with the first recorded data in the 1920s. The general fertility rate is usually considered a more accurate measure but in this period it is only available for 22 states, including only 6 of the experimental group. However, its correlation with the crude birth rate is .97 so we have confidence in the crude rate.

In Table 4-1 we see that the average crude birth rate in the suffrage states is 20.4 and 23.3 in the nonsuffrage states. The difference holds up for the general fertility rate which is 573.4 in the suffrage states and 616.1 in the nonsuffrage states. The latter difference is not statistically significant, though the first difference is. Thus, the hypothesis that the presence of suffrage has a negative impact upon the birth rate is confirmed for one measure and weakly confirmed for the other measure.

Regression Analysis. An inference problem with this type of research design is that the control and experiment groups may differ in some important way and this unmeasured factor may create the observed difference between the two groups. Therefore, we included two of these variables, proportion of females employed in 1920 and proportion of females illiterate in 1920, in a regression equation with a dummy variable for suffrage. As we see in Table 4-2 the results generally confirm our hypothesis and the findings of other scholars. For each birth rate measure, female employment had a negative effect on the birth rate,

Table 4-1

Comparison of Means for Suffrage and Nonsuffrage States

States	Average Crude Birth Rate Mean, 1920s	General Fertility Rate Mean, 1920
Suffrage States (N = 12)	20.4	573.4
Non-suffrage States (N = 36)	23.3	616.1
Difference	2.9[a]	42.7

[a]t-test significant at .05 level.

Source: U.S. Bureau of the Census, "Vital Statistics Rates in the U.S., 1900-1940" (Washington, D.C.: U.S. Government Printing Office, 1956), pp. 666-680.

---

[a]The birth rate measures are lagged because the effect of female status is not instantaneous.

Table 4-2

Regression Results for Birth Rate Equations in States: 1920s

I. Average Crude Birth Rate $\qquad R^2 = .19^a \qquad N = 48$

BR = 23.67 − .0067 Female Employment − 2.73 Suffrage + .15 Illiterate
Stan. Error (.0095) $(1.16)^b$ (9.52)

II. General Fertility Rate $\qquad R^2 = .50^a \qquad N = 22$

BR = 734.20 − 10.56 Female Employment − 15.16 Suffrage + 19.52 Illiterate
Stan. Error $(3.63)^b$ (40.15) $(4.95)^b$

[a]F statistic significant at .05 level

[b]t statistic significant at .05 level

Suffrage = 1 in 12 Suffrage States
$\qquad\quad$ = 0 in 36 Nonsuffrage States

Source: U.S. Bureau of the Census, *Fourteenth Census of the United States* vol. 4 (Washington, D.C.: U.S. Government Printing Office, 1923), p. 47; op. cit., vol. 2, p. 1156.

and illiteracy had a positive effect upon the birth rate. Both equations have respectable R^2's. In the first equation, for average birth rate, suffrage is the only significant variable, i.e., even when female employment and illiteracy are having the desired effects, the presence of suffrage has a significant depressing effect upon the birth rate. In the second equation, for the general fertility rate, suffrage exhibits the desired negative effect but is nonsignificant while the other two variables are significant. Probably the lack of significance for suffrage can be attributed to the fact that only six out of twelve suffrage states are included in the small N of 22.

In sum, the two exercises show female status to be a promising population policy. We have demonstrated that one simple measure of female status, the right to vote, has the hypothesized effect of decreasing the birth rate. In the presence of two other standard variables, suffrage still has a negative effect on birth rate. This relationship is significant for the measure, average crude birth rate, but insignificant for the measure, general fertility rate. Since the two birth rate measures are highly correlated, we presume that the weaker results for the general fertility rate are due to the small number of cases. We also expect that, if a simple dummy variable performs so well, a more refined scale of female status would provide even stronger confirmation of the hypothesis.

In any case we are encouraged about the present case in which women have access to modern contraception. It can be argued that the marginal effect of female status upon the birth rate would be greater than the marginal effect of contraceptive breakthroughs.[19] However, before analyzing the present situation let us pause to consider the present and future status of women in the labor force. Since the motivational explanation requires employment opportunities, let us look at the opportunities for women as they spend less time mothering fewer children.

The Status of Women in
the Labor Market

The size of the female labor force is around 33 million and increasing steadily. The civilian labor force participation rate for adult women (the proportion of women who work or who actually seek employment) moved from 43.1 percent in mid-1971 to 44.4 percent in mid-1973 and is expected to reach 45.5 percent by 1980.[20],[b] The likelihood of a woman's being in the labor force varies: (1) by her marital status—in 1974, 57 percent of single women worked; 43 percent of married women with the husband present worked; and 40.1 percent of widowed, divorced, or separated women worked;[21] (2) by parental status—in 1974, 13.5 million female workers were mothers;[22] and (3) by age of child—slightly more than half of mothers with school age children were in the labor force in 1974; one-third of all mothers with children under six were. The greatest increase has been from mothers with children under three whose labor force participation rate in 1974 was 31 percent.[23]

A crucial place to look for signs of progress in women's employment is in the success of the most recent female college graduates. In a 1974 study of 1972 graduates the women's success rate was spotty: 8.2 percent of the men were still unemployed at the time of the study and 11.0 percent of the women were.[24] More of the women had found work directly related to their field of study. The median earnings of males was $7,574 and of females, $6,681.

Another indicator of different employment opportunities for women lies in the method by which the graduates found their first job. The means of job search that proved to be helpful to more men than women were friends and relatives, private employment, professional periodicals, civil service applications, and public employment services. The sources that helped a higher proportion of women than men were school placement, newspaper advertisement, and direct application to employer (50 percent). Thus, the employed women not only had to get into college, finance their way, and remain in a personal situation that permitted them to look for work (i.e., unmarried, childless, or a permissive husband), but half of them also had to be self-starters in finding their first jobs, which then turned out to pay less than those of the men—not a particularly encouraging situation for feminism or for advocates of population reduction. Furthermore, the effect of the already lowered fertility rate on the supply of jobs projected for 1980 is profound. Coupled with women's rising educational attainment and increased work participation rates, women's demand for jobs will be increasing while these same forces are acting as depressants on the supply side of the job market. The postwar baby boom will result in a 1980 labor force of 102.8 million and, assuming even a two-child average per family, the potential female labor force is expected to increase by 70 percent for the 25-34 age group alone.[25]

---

[b]The same conclusion is supported by economic analyses of fertility.

By the end of the decade 900,000 college graduates are expected in the age group 25-34. There will be more intense competition among women and with men, especially if women remain concentrated in the seventeen occupations where one-half of women now are, instead of being spread throughout sixty-three occupations as males are.[26] There has been little change in sex typing by industry over the last thirty years. The service industry employs the most women (6.8 million) partly because there is a lot of part-time work available.[27] The fastest growing field within this industry is health care, where 80 percent are women. The trade industry ranks second in female employment (6.3 million), mostly in retail sales. In the 1970s job openings in trade are expected to be one-half of the openings of the 1960s. Government agencies rank third in female employment (6.1 million). Most of the women here are in education where job openings are certainly declining. Manufacturing ranks fourth (5.6 million women) but the future job demand is mostly in male dominated fields.

One study of the future of the female labor force has examined the effects of declining fertility and rising educational attainment upon the job market, assuming that women are distributed among occupations as they were in the 1960s.[28] This method furnishes a picture of how women will fare in the job market if there are no advances made into traditionally male occupational roles. The study first makes a projection on the basis of changes in age and educational composition alone (leaving out the effects of lowered fertility). Only in the sales area (the lowest paid) will demand for women exceed supply of women; while in white-collar, professional, clerical, and managerial occupations the female labor supply will exceed job market demand in 1980. The implication of this prediction is that unless women increase their share of higher level blue- and white-collar jobs or unless employment in the female occupations can be expanded more than seems likely, the occupational status of women will deteriorate in the near future.

The study also looked, under the same assumptions, in more detail at ten selected professions that together account for 75 percent of female professional workers. For this group the supply of women workers exceeds demand by 1.2 million and for the college-educated women in this category the supply exceeds the demand by 436,000. Again the implication is that these ten professions simply cannot provide the same job openings for women in the future. One of the professions particularly hard hit is teaching. As a result of the 1.9 fertility rate, the discrepancy between the proportion of people in the teaching age group and the proportion in the student age group is great. It is estimated that after 1976, the average annual increase in demand for college teachers will decline by half.[29]

Finally, the study examined the future job market under a second projection that includes higher work participation rates as an effect of the old 2.1 fertility rate. In this projection, which is even more realistic in its assumptions than the first, the total 1980 demand for women's labor will be 1.75 million less than the supply of available female labor. The indications are that educational attainment and its increased work participation rate will make the situation worse—given the current economic situation and the recent 1.9 fertility rate, our prospects are even gloomier.

Some kinds of major labor market adjustments will have to be made just to maintain the present occupational status of females. To achieve the parity demanded by feminists within the market structure described above will require continued and astute political pressure because new female occupations, in the slow-growth economy we have, may be viewed as coming at the expense of male jobs. Without political, social, and economic change the achievement of a stable population will have been at the expense of women. By having fewer children and thus getting out of the business of motherhood, women may have put themselves out of any business at all. They may become victims of population policy.

The Effect of Female Status
in the Future

Well, enough of the gloom and doom forecasts. An emphasis on family planning with little regard to employment opportunities is self-defeating from a feminist or a demographic perspective. Thus, the present situation is complicated—how to lower population growth when contraceptive technology is quite advanced and its marginal effect is low. It seems to me that a population policy emphasizing female status is the answer for both our society and feminism. A number of current policies might properly be classified as population policy as they may reduce fertility and alter the composition of the population: the Equal Pay Act of 1963, Title VII of the Civil Rights Act of 1964; Executive Order 11373; the Higher Education Act of 1972; and the Women's Equity Education Act of 1974.

The most potentially important policy is the Equal Rights Amendment, passed by Congress in 1972 (after 50 years of consideration) and now awaiting ratification by four more states. It could further reduce fertility through its motivational effect on education and employment and alter the grim future described above. Its simple language encompasses in law, if not in fact, many of the changes feminists have demanded: "Equality of rights under the law shall not be denied or abridged by the United States or by any State on account of sex." As a symbol and as an explicit basis in constitutional law for equality between the sexes, the amendment would go far toward creating a political system in which women would have the maximum incentive and encouragement to live for themselves rather than through motherhood. The Equal Rights Amendment would be a population policy reducing fertility, but not at the expense of women, in contrast to some proposals mentioned earlier.

For this reason the President's Population Commission in its section on women had only one recommendation: that the Congress and the states approve the Equal Rights Amendment and other positive programs to ensure freedom from discrimination based on sex.[30] An examination of the testimony before a subcommittee of the Senate Judiciary Committee shows the Equal Rights Amendment's potential for political change by and for women as well as its potential for population reduction. Several women's leaders testimonies indicate the proposed amendment's relation to population control. Bernice Sandler, a national officer of the Women's Equity Action League, testified that:

We live in a rapidly changing world, one which is threatened by the problems of population growth. There is little reason to expect a woman to limit her family if the only realistic alternative to childbearing is a job far below her capacities, coupled with extension educational and occupational discrimination. Extensive reform in our abortion laws, and the dissemination of birth control information will have little impact unless women have something else to do with their lives. The education of women is crucial if we are to achieve this.[31]

The president of the National Organization for Women, Wilma Scott Heide, spoke in a similar vein:

... our Government must understand that no matter how safe, and universally available is any contraceptive method for women or men, that if women have no viable significant alternatives to motherhood, they will continue to overproduce children instead of being producers of ideas, literature, art, policy, inventions, and leadership. The problem is one of identity, motivation, social climate, legal inequality, and psychological oppression.[32]

Conclusion

Both coercive antinatalism and coercive pronatalism are inimical to women because they seek to mandate reproduction decisions. Voluntary family planning relies too much on technology and overlooks the motivational aspect supplied by female status policies. Motivation towards contraception explains the negative association usually found among fertility and employment and similar variables, whether the analysis is conducted at the individual or national level.

It was argued that female status policies are effective in reducing population growth where there is no contraception available or where contraceptive technology is quite advanced. The first argument was supported by an analysis of the effect of women's suffrage on the birth rate during the 1920s in the American states. The second argument is more speculative but the present lowly status of female labor and the gloomy job prospects for women suggest that female status policies are needed to change compositional characteristics of the female population as well as to reduce population growth.

Notes

1. Virginia Gray, "Women: Victims or Beneficiaries of U.S. Population Policy?" in Virginia Gray and Elihu Bergman, eds., *Political Issues in U.S. Population Policy* (Lexington: Heath/Lexington, 1974). Pp. 167-187.

2. Elihu Bergman, "The Evaluation of Population Policy: Some Missing Links," paper prepared for delivery at the Rehovot Conference on Economic Growth in Developing Countries, Weizmann Institute of Science, Rehovot, Israel, September, 1973, p. 13. Reprinted with permission of Elihu Bergman.

3. Judith Blake, "Coercive Pronatalism and American Population Policy," in U.S. Commission on Population Growth and the American Future, *Aspects of Population Growth Policy*, Vol. VI of Commission Research Reports (Washington: U.S. Government Printing Office, 1972). Pp. 85-114.

4. Kingsley Davis, "Population Policy: Will Current Programs Succeed?" in Edward Pohlman, ed., *Population: A Clash of Prophets* (New York: Mentor, 1973). P. 362.

5. Bernard Berelson, "Beyond Family Planning," in Pohlman, op. cit., pp. 374-407; Edward Pohlman, "The Deadly Desire—For Children," in Pohlman, op. cit., pp. 426-436; Garrett Hardin, "Multiple Paths to Population Control," in Daniel Callahan, *The American Population Debate* (New York: Anchor, 1971). Pp. 259-266; Edgar Chasteen, "The Case for Compulsory Birth Control," in Callahan, op. cit., pp. 274-278.

6. *Spokeswoman* (February 15, 1973), p. 10.

7. *Ms.* 2 (February, 1974), p. 18; *Womanpower* (November, 1973), p. 1.

8. See the critique by J. Richard Udry, *Journal of Marriage and the Family*, 35 (November, 1973), pp. 597-602.

9. Ruth B. Dixon, "Hallelujah the Pill?" *Transaction* 8 (November/December, 1970), p. 48.

10. William Rich, *Smaller Families Through Social and Economic Progress* (Overseas Development Council, 1973). P. 44.

11. T. Paul Schultz, "Economic Determinants of Fertility," in Economic Development Center, *Annual Report: 1974* (St. Paul: University of Minnesota, 1974). P. 8.

12. Robert H. Weller, "The Employment of Wives: Role Incompatibility and Fertility," *Milbank Memorial Fund Quarterly* 46 (July, 1968), p. 251.

13. Edward Pohlman, "The Deadly Desire—For Children," in Pohlman, op. cit., p. 432.

14. Phyllis Chesler, *Women and Madness* (New York: Avon, 1972). Pp. 42-43.

15. Richie H. Reed and Susan McIntosh, "Costs of Children," in U.S., Commission on Population Growth and the American Future, *Economic Aspects of Population Change*, Vol. II of Commission's research reports (Washington: U.S. Government Printing Office, 1972). P. 345.

16. U.S. Commission on Population Growth and the American Future, *Population and the American Future*, report of the Commission (Washington: U.S. Government Printing Office, 1972). P. 87.

17. See for example: Jeanne Clare Ridley, "On the Consequence of Demographic Change for the Roles and Status of Women," in U.S. Commission on Population Growth and the American Future, *Demographic and Social Aspects of Population Growth*, Vol. I of Commission Research reports (Washington: U.S. Government Printing Office, 1972). Pp. 289-304; Suzanne Keller, Ibid., pp. 267-288; Judith Blake, Ibid.; pp. 85-114; Judith Blake, "The Changing Status of Women in Developed Countries," *Scientific American* 231 (September, 1974), pp. 137-147.

18. Peggy R. Sanday, "Toward a Theory of the Status of Women," *American Anthropologist* 75 (October, 1973), pp. 1682-1700.

19. See T. Paul Schultz, "Determinants of Fertility: A Micro Economic Model of Choice," (mimeo) University of Minnesota, 1973.

20. Paul D. Flaim, "Employment Developments in the First Half of 1973," *Monthly Labor Review* 96 (September, 1973), pp. 25-26.

21. Howard Hayghe, "Marital and Family Characteristics of Workers, March 1974," *Monthly Labor Review* 98 (January, 1975), pp. 60-61.

22. Elizabeth Waldman, "Children of Working Mothers, March 1974," *Monthly Labor Review* 98 (January, 1975), p. 64.

23. Hayghe, op. cit., p. 61.

24. Anne M. Young, "Labor Market Experience of Recent College Graduates," *Monthly Labor Review* 97 (October, 1974), p. 33.

25. U.S. Department of Labor, *Manpower Report of the President, 1973* (Washington: U.S. Government Printing Office, 1973). P. 66.

26. U.S. Department of Labor, *Manpower Report of the President, 1974* (Washington: U.S. Government Printing Office, 1974). P. 107.

27. Elizabeth Waldman and Beverly J. McEaddy, "Where Women Work—An Analysis by Industry and Occupation," *Monthly Labor Review* 97 (May, 1974), p. 5.

28. Valerie Kincade Oppenheimer, "Rising Educational Attainment, Declining Fertility and the Inadequacies of the Female Labor Market," in U.S. Commission on Population Growth and the American Future, *Demographic and Social Aspects of Population Growth*, op. cit., p. 315.

29. U.S. Department of Labor, *Manpower Report of the President, 1973*, op. cit., p. 77.

30. U.S. Commission on Population Growth and the American Future, *Population and the American Future*, op. cit., p. 94.

31. Catharine Stimpson, ed., *Women and the "Equal Rights" Amendment: Senate Subcommittee Hearings on the Constitutional Amendment, 91st Congress* (New York: Bowker, 1972), p. 128.

32. Ibid., pp. 194-195.

5

Black Women Officeholders: The Case of State Legislators

Jewel L. Prestage

Throughout the long history of the American political experience, the two largest groups most discriminated against in the political arena have been women and blacks. Black women have the unique distinction of having borne the brunt of both of these discriminatory patterns. In the four-level American political power hierarchy based on race and sex, black women occupy the very lowest position. Despite this disadvantaged status a limited number of black women have succeeded in gaining access to political offices and some have managed to achieve distinction while serving. While this chapter will be primarily devoted to those black women who served as state legislators between 1971 and 1974, a brief introductory section will be devoted to a general overview of the black woman in the American political process.

General Overview

This introductory section will deal with two facets of the black woman in the American political process; namely, the black woman and the political socialization function and the black woman as political participant.

The Black Woman and the Political
Socialization Function

In the main, the scholarly account of the black experience has been through the eyes of white writers.[1] That the legal and customary discrimination against black women has been buttressed by a concomitant body of appropriate literature can be substantiated by a review of such literature by social scientists and popular writers. The central theme in most of the literature is the role of women in the black family. Dominant in this view is the characterization of her role as that of a "matriarch." However, some other themes have also surfaced. One writer, synthesizing role depictions of black women in this literature, identifies three major stereotypes: the matriarchal image; the depreciated sex object image; and the loser image.[2] While all of these stereotypes are relevant to the role of the black female in political socialization, the matriarchal image, no doubt, has the

81

widest implications. This is true because it not only deals with the consequences of the socialization process, but implies something about the female as an agent of socialization in the black family.

Political socialization research findings reveal that black Americans relate to the American system in a different manner than do white Americans.[3] Blacks have displayed a higher level of cynicism and distrust and a lower level of political efficacy. However, efforts to detect major differences in black children and youth along sexual lines have been mostly unsuccessful.

A significant segment of the research efforts on differential attitudes and behavior among black children has focused on the impact of family structure—primarily father absence. As such, the research, then, has focused on the matriarchal image. No major differences have been reported among black American children based on whether or not the father lived in the home.[4] In a related research development, however, some interesting findings have emerged regarding the comparative role of mothers and fathers in the transmission of political values to American children. As reported by John Stucker elsewhere in this volume, these findings suggest that if mothers did once occupy a subordinate role in the process, this has or is changing.[5]

A body of recent scholarly opinion would seem to provide an adequate basis for the rejection of the matriarchal thesis.[6] Sociologists Herbert Hyman and John Shelton Reed have projected the view that there is no more evidence to suggest a matriarchal pattern in black families than in white ones.[7] Summarily, then, with regard to the role of the black woman in the political socialization process, the following generalizations would seem to prevail:

1. the presence or the absence of the father in the black family has made no substantial discernible differences in the political orientations of black American children.
2. no substantial differences have been reported in the political orientations of black boys and girls.
3. the mother in the American family might well be a coequal or even a dominant influence in the transmission of political party identity to children.
4. the matriarchal pattern attributed by many authors to the black family might well be a myth.

The Black Woman as a
Political Participant

In the chapter of this volume, "Women as Voters," some attention has been given to the voting behavior of black women.[a] However, an additional observa-

aBecause the major findings in this area are reviewed in that section, discussion here is limited.

tion on the findings of Professor Marjorie Lansing seems appropriate here. In a study based on 1972 election data, she states "black women, in comparison to black men and both white sexes, held the lowest sense of political efficacy and the lowest levels of trust in the Federal government. Yet the voting record of black women over the last decade shows a rate of increase greater than that of any other sex/race group."[8] Further, the gap in voting between black men and women was less than that of whites, especially for women of elementary education. While black women still trail white women in voting, the recency of the removal of legal barriers to black voting and the accompanying increases are striking.

Officeholding, elective and appointive, is a rather recent occurrence in the lives of blacks, North and South. Regarding the southern scene, Matthews and Prothro stated in a 1966 volume, "Only about 5 percent of all southern counties had one or more Negroes in elective or appointive office from 1945 to 1960."[9] In a somewhat more caustic manner, former United States Attorney General Ramsey Clark, stated to a 1968 conference of about 300 black elected officials from the South, "Four years ago we could have held this meeting in the telephone booth in the lobby and not interfered with anybody who wanted to make a phone call."[10] Southern officeholding by blacks followed the passage of the 1965 Voting Rights Act.

Blacks in the North have experienced fewer legal restraints on political participation than existed in the South. Major participation gains, however, have come in the North only after legal restraints were removed in the South.[11] During this period black officeholding was almost exclusively in the Southern region. Within the increasing number of blacks holding office women have made progressive gains. For example, in a 1964 study, Edward T. Clayton found that the majority of the black political workers were women, who outnumbered men in performing grassroots tasks necessary to political success. Women, nonetheless, did not reap rewards commensurate with their contributions to the party. Only a score or so of women were found to have made a "dramatic success at politics." Less than a dozen had, across the nation, gained elective office at that time. Those who had elevated themselves to positions of power had done so within the political parties. Clayton reports a comment made by the late black congressman and political leader from Chicago, William Dawson—"The Negro woman has been the salvation of Negroes politically ... they are unbending, cannot be easily swayed and cannot be bought."[12]

By 1974 black women held about 337 of the more than 520,000 elective offices in America. The majority were offices related to education, the heaviest concentration by single geographic region was in the South, and the states with the greatest number of black female officeholders also had the greatest cadre of black males elected to office. Black women had been least successful in their bids for positions at the county and federal levels. When women are viewed as a subgroup among black officeholders, they constitute about 12 percent of the group, or 377 out of an estimated 2,991.[13]

Any effort to study the political participation of black women must take into account an observation made by several investigators researching black political behavior. That is, in the face of lack of access of traditional avenues of participation, blacks have resorted to nontraditional avenues.[14] Notable among these nontraditional modes have been voters leagues and protest activities of nonviolent and violent varieties. Women have been very active in voters leagues and studies of protest activities among black college students and adults have documented the significant participation by women.[15] This high level of female presence can be detected from an examination of photographs of protest scenes. A New Orleans study done in 1973, revealed that there were only minimal overall variations in the volume of protest and traditional political participation of black men and women, but women had less positive feeling toward the political system than men.[16]

Volunteer activities for black women have encompassed some of the traditional needs, but have, for the most part, been directed toward fulfilling basic needs of the black community, which have been ignored by the larger political and economic systems. Particularly significant was the work of the benevolent societies designed to provide security in times of illness and death. More recently black women have been active with the National Welfare Rights Organization and the various antipoverty programs. Community services activities and change-oriented activities have been the major volunteer outlets for black women.

Inez Reid's volume, *Together Black Women*,[17] is an indepth study of "so called militant" black women. Professor Reid rejects the label of "militant" in describing these women in favor of "together." A "together" black woman emerges as one who is relatively young, apolitical in the traditional sense, semireligious, working in a variety of jobs, with some college education, highly conscious of her blackness, involved in the black struggle, selfless, fearless, and confident. In addition, these women feel that their interests are dramatically opposed to those of the women's liberation movement and display gross disenchantment with the American political system. They are willing to embrace violence as a viable solution to black oppression.

It is against the backdrop set forth in this section that black women state legislators must be viewed.

Black Women State Legislators

Between 1971 and 1974, 35 black women served in American state legislatures. While 31 served in the lower houses, 4 were in upper houses. The sample on which this study is based includes 32 of these lawmakers. Data in this study were obtained principally through interviews ranging from 45 minutes to 2½ hours, utilizing a 60-item interview schedule. In addition, printed materials were supplied by legislative research agencies in the states and biographical and other printed information was made available by the legislators' offices. Periodicals, statistical data, and professional literature were also consulted.

In this reporting of findings, concern will be limited to the following dimensions of the data assembled:

1. geographic origins and distribution,
2. family background and education,
3. occupation,
4. age,
5. marital status and family size,
6. prior political experience,
7. tenure and future plans, and
8. political party affiliation.

Geographic Origin and Distribution. The 35 black women who served in legislatures were from 23 states while the 32 interviewed were located in 21 states. Table 5-1 provides information on the black population percentage in these states, the number of black women serving in the legislature, and the total black membership of the legislature for the 1970-1972 period and for current terms.

The data suggest that the Midwest is the most fertile territory for females wishing to cultivate careers in legislative service. Blacks seem to have experienced a greater degree of success in those areas where the black percentage of the population is less pronounced. This observation would seem to have interesting research implications reminiscent of V.O. Key's thesis relative to proportion of blacks in the population and black political participation patterns.[18] Other possibilities include racial residential patterns and the politics of reapportionment in these areas.

While the advantage for election seems to lie in the Midwest, the urban South is the region of origin for the greater portion of the women in this study (43.7 percent). Equal portions come from small to moderate sized cities and large cities in the North (21.8 percent from each) and the remaining indicate they grew up in small to moderate sized cities in the South. None grew up in the rural South.

Family Background. Table 5-2 points out the educational levels of the legislators and of the fathers and mothers of the legislators.

Data on education reveal that while 40.5 percent of the fathers and 40.5 percent of the mothers had less than a high school education, this was true of none of the legislators. Further, according to 1972 census data the median school years completed by persons of all races, 25 years or older, was 12.2 and for all women 12.2. A lower figure of 10.3 was the median for all blacks while black women had completed 10.4 years and black men 10.1 years. A minimum

Table 5-1

Black Women Legislators, Total Black Legislators and Black Percentage of Population by States

State	Black Percentage of Population 1970	Black Women Legislators 1972	1974	Total Number of Black Legislators 1972	1974
Arizona	3.0	1	0	4	2
California	7.0	1	0	6	7
Colorado	3.0	0	1	3	4
Connecticut	6.0	0	1	6	6
Delaware	14.3	1	1	3	3
Florida	15.3	1	2	2	3
Georgia	25.8	1	2	15	16
Illinois	12.8	0	1	19	19
Indiana	6.9	0	1	2	7
Iowa	1.2	1	0	1	1
Kentucky	7.2	3	3	3	3
Louisiana	29.8	1	1	8	8
Maryland	17.8	3	3	18	19
Massachusetts	3.1	0	1	3	5
Michigan	11.2	4	3	16	13
Missouri	10.3	2	2	15	15
New Jersey	10.7	1	1	5	7
New York	11.9	0	1	12	14
Oklahoma	6.7	1	1	6	4
Pennsylvania	8.6	1	0	11	13
Tennessee	15.8	0	1	8	9
Texas	12.5	1	2	3	8
Washington	2.1	1	1	3	2
Total		24	29	206	236

Source: U.S. Bureau of the Census, Congressional District Data, Districts of 93 Congress CDD-93X; *National Roster of Black Elected Officials*, vol. 4 (Washington, D.C.: Joint Center for Political Studies, 1974).

of a Bachelors degree is possessed by 52.9 percent of the women in the study. They resemble their white counterparts from a study of women legislators serving in 1963-1964. That author found that most had some form of post-high-school education, but less than half graduated from college.[19]

Occupation. Black women lawmakers represent a variety of occupations and professions as presented in Table 5-3.

Table 5-2
Education of Legislators and Fathers and Mothers of Legislators (in Percentages)

Educational Level	Fathers	Mothers	Legislators
Some Elementary	18.7	6.2	—
Elementary Completed	21.8	34.3	—
High School Completed	18.7	28.1	—
Special/Vocational Postsecondary	—	—	12.5
Attended College	6.2	12.5	34.3
Bachelors Degree	21.8	15.6	31.2
Masters Degree	—	—	9.3
Law Degree	—	—	9.3
Ph.D., M.D., D.D.S., or Equivalent	6.2	—	3.1
Failed to Respond	6.2	3.1	—

Table 5-3
Occupation/Profession of Legislators

Occupation/Profession	Number of Legislators
College Professor	1
Lawyer	3
Teacher	3
Librarian	1
Social Worker	5
Journalist	1
Nurse	3
Businesswoman (owner of)	6
Managers	2
Clerical	2
Consultant/Public Relations Specialist	2
Housewife	1
Incomplete Response	2

Multiendeavors were very common among respondents. For example, one legislator held a college degree, had been a teacher, a secretary, a social worker with the Red Cross overseas, and now publishes a newspaper. Another held a Masters degree, a law degree, and had pursued a professional life that included teaching, a school principalship, and law. Another had been a classroom teacher of French, a research biochemist, and Law Librarian for the state. Categorization was based on the profession to which the respondent indicated greater allegiance or in which service had been longest.

Age. Legislators' ages ranged from 20 to 70 with the majority over 40. This is consistent with earlier studies of women in Congress and state legislatures. Because of the use of age ranges rather than specific age in the interview instrument, no average age can be computed. However, the youngest legislator was 29 and the oldest retired after her 70th birthday, with 18 years of legislative service. Table 5-4 gives the age levels.

Marital Status and Family Size. Compatibility between public officeholding and family life for women has long been a matter of concern and speculation. Less than half of the women (49.9 percent) are either presently married or widowed.

Of the 12 divorced women, 5 were divorced prior to campaigning for office and 3 others disclaimed any relationship between political endeavors and divorce. One of 2 legal separations reported is directly attributable to conflict over political officeholding. Marital status is shown in Table 5-5.

Family Size. The number of children ranged from 10 women with no children to one with 7 children. Overall distribution is given in Table 5-6.

About two-thirds of the legislators are mothers. When legislators are grouped on the basis of children's ages, only 15 percent have children under 18 years. Some research implications of findings on family size and marital status will be considered below.

Table 5-4
Age Ranges of Legislators

Age Group	Percentages
20-30 years	6.2
31-40 years	25.0
41-50 years	34.4
51-60 years	15.6
Over 60 years	18.7

Table 5-5
Marital Status of Black Women Legislators

Marital Status	Percentage
Single	6.2
Married	34.3
Divorced	37.5
Widowed	15.6
Legally Separated	6.2

Table 5-6
Number of Children in Families of Black Women Legislators

Number of Children Had	Percentage
No Children	31.2
One Child	18.7
Two Children	21.8
Three Children	15.6
Four Children	6.2
Five Children	None
Six Children	3.1
Seven Children	3.1

Prior Political Experience. Studies of the United States Congress indicate that until rather recently most women members have come as replacements to serve out terms to which their husbands had been elected.[20] This pattern has also prevailed at the state level. Among these black lady lawmakers, only one had initial service as a replacement for her husband who had died in office. She subsequently sought and won election to this position in her own right. Another replaced her husband when he withdrew as party nominee following a primary victory. The remaining women came to office with no special advantage related to their husbands holding the office previously.

For 40 percent of these women, their first term in the legislature represented their maiden venture into the political arena. Table 5-7 presents data on this question.

In Table 5-8 a picture of the women's views of their expertise and special competence upon entering the legislature for the first time is given.

Tenure in Office and Future Plans. Of the 29 women currently in office, 11 are serving their initial terms. The fate of the 24 legislators who ended terms in 1972

Table 5-7
Political Experience of Black Women Legislators

Type Experience	Percentage
Elective Office	9.3
Appointive Office	18.7
Salaried Employee	6.2
Political Party Position	21.8
Civil Rights Organizations	3.1
None	40.6

Table 5-8
Views of Personal Expertise and Special Competence by Black Women Legislators

Response	Percentage
Yes, Special Expertise	84.3
No	12.5
Uncertain	3.1

was as follows: 2 were elected Congresswomen, 2 retired, 1 was defeated when her old district was eliminated, 1 was defeated when she decided not to seek reelection to the House but to run for a Senate seat, and 18 were reelected.

The average length of service for the 18 incumbents in the legislatures now is 6.8 years. One of the retirees in 1972 had served for 18 consecutive years in her state house.

It is estimated that close to one-half of the approximately 7,600 American state legislators are replaced every two years, primarily because incumbent legislators refuse to seek reelection.[21] Probing of these legislators relative to reelection plans netted the results shown in Table 5-9.

Because of the recency of black women holding legislative posts, any suggestions about upward mobility prospects and possibilities would seem premature. However, Joseph Schlesinger contends that "Ambition lies at the heart of politics. Politics thrives on the hope of preferment and drive for office."[22] To what extent do black women lawmakers aspire for higher office? Table 5-10 reveals their responses when asked this question.

A general level of ambivalence seems to be reflected as these data are studied. Noteworthy, however, is the knowledge that 3 of the 4 black Congresswomen are former state legislators.

In a related inquiry, the women were asked to give their opinions on the future of blacks in American politics, of women in American politics, and of the Women's Liberation Movement. Generally optimistic views on the former two emerged as seen in Table 5-11.

Table 5-9
Reelection Plans for Black Women State Legislators

Response	Percentages
No Response	3.1 (1)
Yes	71.8 (23)
No	3.1 (1)
Uncertain	15.6 (5)
Retired	6.2 (2)

Table 5-10
Ambitions for Higher Office of Black Women Legislators

	Responses	Percentages
	Yes	31.2
	No	31.2
	Uncertain	31.2
	Retired	6.2

Table 5-11
Views on Future of Women in Politics and Blacks in Politics

Opinion	Future of Blacks (%)	Future of Women (%)
Very Bright	53.1	71.8
Moderately Bright	28.1	15.6
Not Very Bright	12.5	6.2
Uncertain	6.2	6.2

Numerous black women have articulated views on the Women's Liberation Movement and its relevance to their interests. For the woman legislator the most widespread attitude is that the movement has some merits but must be accorded very low status among their policy priorities. Table 5-12 reveals results on this question.

One of the respondents who is skeptical of the Women's Liberation Movement said "Women's liberators scream for equality. With the majority vote in the hands of women, women vote men into office. Evidently they don't want to be liberated." Further, she continued "Who is to be liberated from what? To what? White women from homes while black women take care of their kids."

A more typical view was that of a legislator who assessed the movement in these words, "It is good and bad. Good in areas of employment and profession ... black women haven't been turned on to it because we have always worked and have no need to identify. Biggest fight for blacks is racism. NOW and other women's groups will not work for black issues like busing."

Table 5-12
Views on Women's Liberation by Black Women Legislators

	Views	Percentages
	Pro, High Priority	15.6
	Pro, Low Priority	53.1
	Neutral	18.7
	Anti	12.5

One of the lady lawmakers with a very good record of support and visibility in the struggle for women's rights remarked "Being a person believing in equality for all, I support Women's Lib but it's not my top priority."

The northern urban lady legislators dominate both ends of the continuum with Southern legislators tending to be less polarized on the question.

Political Party Affiliation. All of the women who served between 1970 and 1974 were Democrats. In their respective bodies, some 71 percent of them served where theirs was the majority party and 25 percent in the minority party.

Conclusions

Gains in officeholding by black women have paralleled those of black men, in that black women served in only one legislature in which there were no black men between 1971 and 1974. That is a state where three black women, at one time, made up 100 percent of the black representation and 100 percent of the female representation. Three of the four black women senators were without either white female colleagues or black male colleagues. These are the only instances that were reported where the black woman legislator experienced such extreme isolation from her race and gender.

Most of the women grew up in moderate to large size cities, primarily in the South. The women are more concentrated outside the South and all of them represent urban districts. As a group they are comparatively well-educated, much like white women legislators. Occupation-wise, the group is made up of women with multiendeavors, about 90 percent having pursued careers outside the home.

Black lady legislators are mostly above the age of 40, are now or were once married, have children, and did not enter politics following the demise of politician husbands. Only a fraction have had prior experience in elective office and 40 percent show no significant political experience in the traditional sense. However, over 80 percent felt that they brought to legislative service some unusual experience or expertise that gave them special advantage in some policy areas.

One means by which power is acquired in American legislative bodies is "longevity in service." Black women, on the average, have only brief tenure in office. Only four exceed ten years of service. Potential reapportionment problems are uppermost in their minds, as they are in urban areas, mostly predominantly black districts. If the women have their wishes, most will establish seniority (as they plan to run again) or go on to higher office. In most instances the involved women are in the majority party in their respective houses. A reasonable prognosis would seem to be that these women will gain seniority in the absence of serious setbacks involving redistricting.

The typical black lady lawmaker views Women's Lib with reservations but feels that the future is bright for both women and blacks in American politics.

Research Implications

The participation gap between black females and the dominant white population is no more pronounced than the knowledge gap regarding their participation. Preliminary findings on black female legislators would seem to point out a need for further exploration in several areas, some of which are among the ongoing research activities of this writer.

1. There is a need to explore the criteria necessary for "effectiveness" on the part of black women legislators. What are the traits that will enable black women legislators (with double minority status) to represent their constituents, "acting in the interests of the represented, in a manner responsive to them."[2][3] Are these traits more akin to those needed by white women legislators or those required of black male legislators for similar levels of "effectiveness." Central to this question of effectiveness are the policy priorities of the legislators as they relate to the needs of the black community or the female community. Several quotes from the women in the study suggest the problems they encounter in this regard:

"White colleagues attribute racial overtones to all my bills regardless of their content."

Another such comment is "If you expect to be effective you must learn compromise, negotiation, trade-offs. This sometimes entails giving up and supporting legislation contrary to your district's interest in exchange for something your district needs."

A Southern lady states "women must work quietly and effectively and take power."

Rather frustrated, another points out that of over 175 members in her chamber "only 14 are blacks, you cannot be very effective on issues involving blacks when you are so few in number."

From a Northern state lawmaker "Blacks get their share of committee assignments but when it comes to getting needed legislation (for example in education) racism is quite obvious. Most obvious on bread and butter issues. Whites just will not support these. Maybe we could do a better job with the 13 voters we have."

Another dimension of the criteria for effectiveness is the legislators' view of the impact of race and sex on her policy and mobility goals. One legislator in a very optimistic view states:

"Being a good legislator is sexless and raceless. One should not view race or sex as an inhibiting factor. We know there is discrimination on the basis of race and sex. . . . Do not feel self-inhibited by factors of race and sex. First, free your mind and your own self-concept. You will find barriers which are *real* and *practical* can be made to disappear."

Another, in an opposing stance, declares "I think it is being black and advocating blackness that held me back. However, if you are formidable they must figure how to get around you."

One of the members of an upper house says "Being black is no different in the senate than in real life. If you let yourself be discriminated against you will be."

To what extent do "effectiveness" criteria for "together" black women (women engaged in nontraditional politics) carry over into the traditional arena?

Perhaps the most critical question arising out of this preliminary analysis is, in this writer's opinion, the need to extract from available information on the legislative process the major basis for the lack of effectiveness in achievement of legislative policy goals on the part of black women. Is it because the proponents are female or black or is it because these female and black legislators do not know the intricacies of the legislative process necessary to sophisticated maneuvering in the chambers? Or, is it possible that black and female legislators adopt policy priorities that would be rejected even if offered by white male legislators? If the answer lies with the former then one set of socialization and skill goals may be appropriate, while if it is the latter, alternatives to electoral politics might be a more feasible scheme.

Further, male legislative effectiveness is usually determined by the extent to which such legislators are successful in getting their policy preferences translated into legislative enactments. Because black women legislators have not had great success in this area, have they been ineffective and without significant impact on the legislative process?

2. A second promising research direction seems to lie in the general area of "ambition theory," the central assumption of which is that politicians respond to their office goals. Politicians act in a manner they consider appropriate to the achievement of office. Ambition theory is devoted to what is termed "the source of politics, the ambitions of politicians."[24] The recency of the entry of black women into electoral politics in measurable numbers would seem to open interesting research possibilities in this direction.

3. Role flexibility among males and females has received a measure of attention in several volumes on the black family.[25] Exploration of the family lives of black women officeholders might be of great heuristic value for other female officeholders, especially as these relate to childbearing and child rearing.

4. There is a need for new research concepts and techniques for defining the

political experiences of women. What is "political" might well need rethinking. For example, is the mother or female social worker involved in the intricacies of the welfare system over a period of years any less experienced in politics than a male who wears a campaign button or gives money to a candidate for office? Many politicizing experiences of women are possibly not recognized as such by current standards. Why, for example, do black women legislators view themselves as having some special expertise based on prior experiences in the absence of prior involvement in what we normally regard as political activity?

5. Finally, it would seem that the prime need is for the generation of additional data on black males in legislative and other offices, black women in nonlegislative elective offices, and comparative data on white female officeholders. In 1974 there were approximately 412 white women state legislators, according to the National Women's Political Caucus and 207 black male state legislators according to the Joint Center for Political Studies.

Notes

1. An interesting discussion of this question is set forth in Mack H. Jones and Alex W. Willingham, "The White Custodians of the Black Experience," *Social Science Quarterly* 51 (June, 1970), pp. 31-36.

2. Mae C. King, "The Politics of Sexual Stereotypes," *The Black Scholar* 4 (March/April, 1973), pp. 12-23.

3. See, for example, Dwaine Marvick, "The Political Socialization of the American Negro," *The Annals of the American Academy of Political and Social Science* 361 (September, 1965), pp. 112-127; Joan Laurence, "White Socialization: Black Reality," *Psychiatry* 33 (May, 1970), pp. 174-194; Schley Lyons, "The Political Socialization of Ghetto Children: Efficacy and Cynicism," *Journal of Politics* 32 (May, 1970), pp. 288-304; Paul Abramson, "Political Efficacy and Political Trust Among Black School Children: Two Explanations," *Journal of Politics* 34 (November, 1972), pp. 1234-1275.

4. However, some reports on non-American families have found differences in this regard. See, for example, Kenneth P. Langton, *Political Socialization* (New York: Oxford University Press, 1969).

5. M. Kent Jennings and Kenneth P. Langton, "Mothers versus Fathers: The Formation of Political Orientations Among Young Americans," *Journal of Politics* 31 (May, 1969), pp. 329-358.

6. See, for example, Robert Staples, "The Myths of Black Matriarchy," *The Black Scholar* 50 (January/February, 1970), pp. 9-16.

7. Herbert H. Hyman and John Shelton Reed, "Black Matriarchy Reconsidered: Evidence From Secondary Analyses of Sample Surveys," *Public Opinion Quarterly* 33 (Fall, 1969), pp. 346-354.

8. Majorie Lansing, "The Voting Pattern of American Black Women," a

paper presented to the 1973 Annual Meeting of the American Political Science Association, New Orleans, Louisiana, September 1973.

9. Donald R. Matthews and James W. Prothro, *Negroes and the New Southern Politics* (New York: Harcourt, Brace & World, 1966), p. 176.

10. Ramsey Clark, "Equal Justice to all Its People," in Southern Regional Council, *Conference Proceedings: Southwide Conference of Black Elected Officials, December 11-14, 1968* (Atlanta: Southern Regional Council, 1968).

11. For a discussion of Black officeholding in the South during Reconstruction see John Hope Franklin, *From Slavery to Freedom* 3rd ed. (New York: Knopf, 1967), pp. 315-323.

12. Edward T. Clayton, *The Negro Politician: His Success and Failure* (Chicago: Johnson, 1974), pp. 122-148.

13. Herrington Bryce and Allan Warrick, "Black Women in Electoral Politics," *Focus* 1 (August 1973).

14. For a good account of these developments see Matthews and Prothro, op. cit., Chapter 8.

15. Among the studies of Black student protest activity are Donald R. Matthews and James Prothro, "Negro Students and the Protest Movement," op. cit., pp. 407-440; Freddye Hill, "Black Nationalism: A Case Study at a Predominantly White Northern University," (Ph.D. dissertation, Northwestern University, Department of Sociology, 1974); E.C. Harrison, "Student Unrest on the Black College Campus," *Journal of Negro Education* 41 (Spring, 1972), pp. 113-120; John Orbell, "Protest Participation Among Southern Negro College Students," *American Political Science Review* 61 (June, 1967), pp. 446-456.

16. John Pierce, William Avery, and Addison Carey, Jr., "Sex Differences in Black Political Beliefs and Behavior," *American Journal of Political Science* 17 (May, 1973), pp. 422-430.

17. Inez Reid, *Together Black Women* (New York: Emerson Hall, 1972).

18. V.O. Key, Jr. *Southern Politics* (New York: Knopf, 1949).

19. Emmy E. Werner, "Women in the State Legislatures," *Western Political Quarterly* 21 (March, 1968), pp. 40-50.

20. Martin Gruberg, *Women in American Politics* (Oshkosh: Academia, 1968).

21. Daniel R. Grant and H.C. Nixon, *State and Local Government in America* (Boston: Allyn & Bacon, 1968), p. 242.

22. Joseph Schlesinger, *Ambition and Politics: Political Careers in the United States* (Chicago: Rand McNally, 1966), p. 1.

23. Hanah Pitkin, *The Concept of Representation* (Berkeley: University of California Press, 1967), pp. 154-155.

24. Joseph Schlesinger, op. cit., pp. 194-195.

25. See for example Robert Hill, *The Strengths of Black Families* (New York: Emerson Hall, 1972); Andrew Billingsley, *Black Families in White America* (Englewood Cliffs, New Jersey: Prentice-Hall, 1968) and Robert Staples *The Black Family: Essays and Studies* (Belmont, California: Wadsworth, 1971).

Women as Voters: Their Maturation as Political Persons in American Society

John J. Stucker

The point of departure for this discussion is the well-known observation that there are very few women who occupy professional roles in the American political system. This observation remains true whether one defines professional political roles as those of party leadership, elected office, appointed office, or the policy-making levels of federal and state civil services. Examples of this situation abound. Another chapter in this volume is devoted to a discussion of black women legislators, a category that counted no more than 35 members during the period 1971-1973. Even if we were to drop the adjective black, we are still left with a miserly number of women elected to representative office. As Krause notes, the federal and state legislative assemblies in this nation consisted of no more than 3 percent women during the quarter century following World War II.[1]

The most recent figures released by the Women's Political Caucus seem to suggest some progress. When the legislatures of the fifty states convened in January of 1975, 604 of their members, or 7.98 percent of the whole, were women. But according to Murphy the pace of change has been and remains glacial.[2] As one example, Professor Murphy points out that at the current rate of recruitment and placement of women into the top 100,000 federal jobs, it will take women 150 years to fill even 25 percent of those positions. Indeed, in summarizing her recent review of the literature on women in politics for the *American Political Science Review*, Professor Krause seems resigned to the conclusion that the more things have changed the more they have remained the same.[3]

Why is it that women have been so slow to participate in professional political roles? The answer is, of course, that there are a multitude of factors—social, economic and cultural—all of which have inhibited women from becoming involved in virtually all types of professional roles. In addition there is the political dimension. The political history of women in the United States, particularly in their role as voters, has had important consequences for their current status within the political system, and it is this subject that will be the focus of the following discussion.

The traditional literature on participatory political cultures has characterized political participation as an essentially intransitive hierarchy of behaviors in which voting serves as the baseline.[4] According to this model, participation in higher-order political roles is dependent on the development of stable and mature patterns of voting, since the motivation for political activism must be nurtured by the politicizing effects of consistent voting. In the case of women in the American political system, this conventional schematic has only limited application. Clearly, women were barred from virtually all political roles during the period in which they did not hold the franchise. On the other hand, once they were formally inducted into the electorate, not all women wanted to or were realistically able to vote; nor did this legal opportunity to vote lead in step-wise fashion to entrance into professional political activism.

Accordingly, the purpose of this chapter will be twofold. In the first instance, we will review the history of women's political status in the United States with particular emphasis on the struggle to gain full suffrage rights for women and the psychological and behavioral responses that characterized their induction into the electorate. Secondly, we will explore how the reaction of various groups of women to their status as political persons has led to variations in the predisposition of women to become professionally involved in politics.

Legal History of Women's Political Status

During the colonial period in North America women had, on the face of it, no political status. With few exceptions the franchise qualifications of the several colonies contained no references to sex as a criterion for eligibility.[5] It might be presumed from all this that women in those days were so conscious of what their proper role in society was that they did not need the benefit of the blunt legal reminders that were to confront the women who followed them. In point of fact, however, it is doubtful that the matter was left quite so much to chance. More than likely the combination of suffrage qualifications based on proper ownership and the statutory laws excluding most women from the ownership of property provided all the legal means necessary to bar women from the franchise. As John Stuart Mill pointed out, lawmakers have seldom relied upon the forces of nature to insure that women remain in their naturally subordinate role.[6]

As the young United States approached the start of the nineteenth century, the ideals that had been embodied in the fight for independence began to appear in the laws of the states. In the case of voting qualifications this took the form of the gradual weakening and subsequent dismantling of requirements based on wealth or property ownership. But in at least one respect, the lawmakers adhered very closely not only to the spirit but also to the letter of the American Revolution. The Declaration of Independence had said that "all *men* are created equal," and, therefore, one by one, the states inserted the word "male" into their rules defining an eligible elector. As Seymour and Frary noted, this first major movement toward national democracy and the universal suffrage would obviously be limited to white males, a policy to be repeated in the wake of the French Revolution.[7]

Before long, however, the first step was taken to extend a limited political role to women. In 1838, Kentucky granted the franchise in school elections to "widows with children of school age in country districts." For almost a quarter of a century Kentucky stood alone with its grant of voting rights to women, but in 1861 Kansas followed suit and during the next fifty years almost two dozen states granted school suffrage to women. One of the more interesting aspects about this phenomenon was that it was national in scope; states in every region of the country participated in this initial extension of the franchise to women as shown in Table 6-1. This contrasts with the decidedly regional bias in the granting of full suffrage rights to women around the turn of the century. Most of the states that made women full-fledged electors prior to the adoption of the 19th Amendment were located in the western United States.

Aside from the fact that this legal status in relation to the voting process was extremely limited, however, a more important point was that it did not involve assigning women a real political role. Their participation in the political system

Table 6-1
Dates When School Suffrage Grants to Women Were Made Effective by State Legislative Action or Change of State Constitution

Date	State
1838	Kentucky
1861	Kansas
1875	Michigan, Minnesota
1876	Colorado
1878	New Hampshire, Oregon
1879	Massachusetts
1880	Mississippi, New York, Utah
1883	Nebraska
1887	Arizona, Kansas, New Jersey, South Dakota
1889	Montana, North Dakota
1890	Oklahoma, Washington
1893	Connecticut
1894	Iowa, Ohio
1900	Wisconsin
1908	Michigan
1910	New Mexico

Source: Adapted from Mildred Adams, et al., *Victory: How Women Won It* (New York: Wilson, 1940), pp. 165-166.

was viewed rather as an extension of a woman's special role in society as a mother and educator of her children. This perspective was most eloquently embodied in the statutes granting school suffrage to women only in the event that they became widows. Presumably, prior to that circumstance, a woman would not need to vote since her motherly concern for the youth of society could be transmitted into the public education system by her asking her husband to exercise his political rights. Needless to say, the suffragists were incensed with the state of affairs.[8]

The women who met in Seneca Falls, New York, in the summer of 1848 and who subsequently founded the National Women Suffrage Association had laid out a program for reform that was not just visionary but in fact radical.[9] Their proposals called for sweeping revisions of the laws, mores, and institutions that kept women in a subordinate role in society. In the political domain, they demanded that women be treated as political persons, not as political mothers. The move by the states to grant school suffrage to women not only did not comply with their demands, it actually served to reemphasize the nature of women as second class citizens.

Beyond the symbolism of this legal change, however, this type of private political role failed to provide women with an experiential basis that would advance the politicization of American women. A number of students of nineteenth century American electoral processes argue that local politics in the last century generated much more interest and participation on the part of the citizenry than has been demonstrated in the findings of mid-twentieth century survey research.[10] While we may concede merit to their arguments, it is still hard to conceive that this partial suffrage grant would have the same politicizing effect on women as would a full grant of suffrage rights.

In research on the adoption of women's suffrage in the United States, it was found that the number of years during which women enjoyed school suffrage had no discernible impact on the direction and amount of change that can be observed in several indices of presidential and congressional voting behavior subsequent to the full enfranchisement of women.[11] In other words, those women who had had the opportunity to vote in school board elections seemed no more likely to vote in national elections once the occasion presented itself than women who were confronting the ballot box for the first time. This was so because in great measure women had not exercised their rights to school suffrage; and, consequently, they had not developed maturity and experience as political persons.

To make matters worse, the legacy of school suffrage eventually became a Catch-22 trap for the advocates of full suffrage rights. By the turn of the century the opponents of women suffrage were arguing that American women had already shown that they were incapable of fulfilling private political roles given their poor levels of participation in school board elections. Of course, women would never be able to prove their capabilities as political persons until they had

had a sustained and meaningful opportunity to act out private political roles—i.e. with full suffrage rights. But the anti's persisted. Why, they argued, should women be given full suffrage rights when they had not shown their ability to exercise even the limited franchise bestowed upon them in so many states.[1][2]

Eventually, the suffragists prevailed, but it was not a quick or easy victory. Their first substantial breakthrough came in 1869 when Wyoming was established as a territory with a proviso guaranteeing equal suffrage rights for all adults. In 1890 it was Wyoming that once again led the way as it entered statehood with a constitution maintaining this principle of universal suffrage. For the first time a state had granted women the right to vote for all elective offices—local, state and national. Within the next six years three more states—Colorado, Idaho, and Utah—had followed Wyoming's lead, but in the decade following 1900 no further progress was made.

After 1910, the ferment over women suffrage began to bubble once again. The reform spirit of Progressivism had established itself within the body politic and the suffragists had now become successful in identifying their ideals and principles with those of the Progressives. As Table 6-2 shows, almost a dozen states had granted full voting rights to women before the decade was out, and in addition twelve other states made the fundamental concession of granting women the right to vote in presidential elections. Finally, in 1919, the U.S. Congress proposed an amendment prohibiting the denial of the right to vote on

Table 6-2
Full and Presidential Suffrage Rights to Women Made Effective by Legislative Action or Constitutional Change at the State Level

Full Suffrage Rights		Presidential Suffrage Rights	
Effective Date	State	Effective Date	State
1890	Wyoming	1913	Illinois
1893	Colorado	1917	Nebraska
1896	Utah		North Dakota, Rhode Island
1897	Idaho	1919	Indiana, Iowa, Minnesota, Ohio, Tennessee, Wisconsin, Missouri
1911	California Washington		
1913	Arizona, Kansas, Oregon		
1915	Montana, Nevada	1920	Kentucky
1917	New York		
1918	Michigan, Oklahoma, South Dakota		

the basis of sex. In marked contrast to the current situation surrounding the Equal Rights Amendment ratification effort, affirmative action by the requisite number of states (36) was swift in coming and on August 25, 1920, Secretary of State Bainbridge Colby signed the proclamation of the 19th Amendment to the Constitution of the United States.

Women's Response to the Legal Change in Their Political Status

The old adage that "you can't legislate morality" seems to summarize a good deal of what we know about the nature of behavioral responses to structural change. Often individuals are slow to modify their attitudes or behaviors to conform with changes in the legal or institutional frameworks impinging upon them. A classic example within recent memory has been the response of the nation, not just the southern states, to the Supreme Court's *Brown* decision and the legion of lower federal court decisions that have followed. The reality of integrated and equal educational opportunities for all has unfolded very slowly across these past two decades.

The enfranchisement of women in western democracies during the late nineteenth and early twentieth centuries was also a situation in which the target group responded rather slowly to their new legal opportunities. While the pattern varied from country to country, available evidence indicates that women voted at consistently lower rates than men. In an early study of voting behavior in western nations, Tingsten reported that the differences in the rates of participation for men and women were as low as 5-7 percent in New Zealand and as high as 25 percent in Iceland, with differences of 10-15 percent in countries such as Germany, Sweden, Finland and Norway.[13] Since voter registers and election results were not reported separately for men and women in the United States, Tingsten could not present the same analysis for this country.

On the basis of the available evidence, however, he suggested that the differential was quite large; and Chafe, citing some limited data from Chicago and New York City, has shown that in the early twenties men were outvoting women in general and local elections by as much as a two-to-one margin.[14] Furthermore, this pattern does not seem to have been limited either to the decade of the twenties nor to these two cities. In my own research I found that, regardless of the year in which full voting rights were granted to women, the average turnout across all the states in both presidential and off-year congressional voting declined by 10 percent points between the two elections immediately preceding and the two elections immediately following the enfranchisement of women in each state.[15]

Why were many women so slow to respond to the political opportunity that some had fought so long and so hard for? Several factors seem to have been operative. For one thing there was a problem of logistics. With the 19th Amendment ratified less than three months before the general election of 1920, there were numerous cases in which local election officials were hard pressed to enroll women in the voting registers and provide adequate numbers of ballots and polling stations. In fact, Gosnell reports, in three states the legislatures did not enact the necessary legislation to permit women to register in time for the 1920 election.[16] Timing and logistics, of course, can not explain all the variance, particularly in those states that enfranchised women prior to 1920.

A second, and clearly more important, factor had to do with race. During the turn of the century when women were finally gaining full access to the ballot box, a movement was underway in the southern states to reverse whatever limited suffrage gains had been made earlier on the part of black men. As Key and others have noted, this effort to disenfranchise blacks had consisted of a variety of extra-legal stratagems and had been underway for some time before the 1890s.[17] It was, however, during this decade that the southern system of election codes was adopted in state after state across the South. These codes, which featured most prominently poll taxes, literacy tests, and long durational residency requirements, helped to seal the fate of black voters throughout this region of the country and subsequently nullified the effects of the 19th Amendment for southern black women.[18]

As for white women, both northern and southern, how do we explain their reaction to being inducted into the electorate? McPhee has articulated a life-cycle model based on learning theory which, if converted to a generational model, can be used not only to explain the behavioral response of white women but also to interpret some empirical data available on early twentieth century voting patterns of the American electorate.[19] Like any behavior, the act of voting can become a pattern or a habit, the maintenance of which an individual can support internally. Developing a habit, however, requires both time and experience. When one is initially confronted with the opportunity to vote, the nature of the behavioral response will be strongly influenced by external cues.

Thus, when women as a group were inducted into the electorate, we would expect their behavior to be governed not so much by the legalities of the situation but rather by their norms and expectations regarding legitimate behavior. In this respect, many women must have felt severe inhibitions about the legitimacy of their voting. For one thing, since no women had been able to vote before the law was changed (discounting the effects of school suffrage), there was no overt role model after which to pattern one's behavior. Furthermore, there was a substantial array of social norms and arguments emphasizing women's role in society as domestic rather than political. These cultural cues would have been particularly influential among middle-aged and older women whose views regarding women in politics were formed without the benefit of the countervailing cues that were generated as the debate over women suffrage reached a climax in the first two decades of this century. Thus, while some women immediately took up the franchise, many others, especially those who had been isolated from the consciousness-raising effects of the suffrage movement, remained at home on election day.

Dramatic evidence of this pattern was offered by Merriam and Gosnell in their study of the 1920 general election and the 1923 mayoralty race in Chicago.[20] These analysts found that while native-born women, particularly those living in the Gold Coast section along the north shore, voted at rates only slightly lower than those of men in general, the participation rate among ethnic women was substantially lower than the male rate. The results from their survey interviews made it clear that immigrant women were far more likely to express the belief that a woman's place was in the home, while it was the man's business to attend to public affairs. This same pattern has been corroborated in my own research. Looking at the same percentage comparison, cited earlier for the nation as a whole, I have found that in the Great Lakes and northeastern regions of the country average turnout in presidential and off-year congressional voting declined from 13 to 17 percent between the two elections before and the two elections after the enactment of women suffrage (see Table 6-3). Since these were the regions of the nation in which the largest number of immigrants were concentrated, it is not surprising that these difference scores were 4 to 7 percent above the national values.

Another example of the effects of social norms is contained in the findings regarding the decline in turnout in the southern states. In this region of the country the percentage decline in presidential turnout was equal to the nation as a whole, ten points. On the face of it this may not appear to be an unusual

Table 6-3

Percentage Point Difference Scores on Four Electoral Indices, Differences Between Two Elections Before and Two Elections After Women Suffrage, National and Five Regions

	Turnout		Mobilization	
	Presidential	Off-Year Congressional	President	Off-Year Congressional
National	−.101	−.108	.168	.104
Northeast	−.134	−.151	.188	.127
Midwest	−.135	−.174	.226	.105
Plains	−.105	−.105	.221	.156
South	−.091	−.064	.050	.014
West	−.011	−.036	.211	.153

Source: Adapted from John J. Stucker, *The Impact of Woman Suffrage on Patterns of Voter Participation in the United States: Quasi-Experimental and Real-Time Analyses, 1890-1920* (Ph.D. dissertation, University of Michigan, 1973), tables 21 and 24.

finding, but one must remember that by 1920 the South had undergone three decades of steep and continuing declines in voter turnout. Thus, just prior to the enfranchisement of women, turnout had declined to such a low ebb that only wholesale abstentions by women on election day could have driven the value of the index down by as much as ten points. While the matrix of poll taxes and literacy tests served to exclude black women from voting participation, it seems clear that the "magnolia curtain" proved to be almost as powerful a barrier in preventing southern white women from exercising their franchise.

Additional evidence of the abstention of southern women from the voting process can be obtained by looking at the other index of electoral behavior in Table 6-3, the mobilization index. In contrast to the turnout index, which measures the total-votes-cast divided by the number of eligible electors, the mobilization index measures the number of votes cast over the total adult population. Thus, while the denominator of the turnout index changes after women are enfranchised (on the average we would expect it to double), the denominator of the mobilization remains constant in its composition. Where we would expect the turnout index to decline after women are enfranchised, we would expect the mobilization index to increase somewhat, reflecting the impact of those women who do begin to vote immediately. (All this is assuming that the participation rate of men is constant—an assumption not always valid.) While the mobilization index for the nation as a whole increased 17 percent for presidential voting and 10 percent for off-year congressional voting after women were given the vote, in the south the mobilization index increased by only 5 and 1 percent respectively for presidential and off-year congressional voting.

In at least one area of the country, however, it appears as though the mechanism of social norms did not operate to repress women from an immediate exercise of their right to vote—the western states. As the results in Table 6-3 indicate, the decline in presidential and congressional turnout was negligible. It could be argued that this result is an artifact of arithmetic. While the sex ratio in the rest of the country more nearly approximated 50-50, in the western states the female proportion of the adult population was about 30 percent during the 1890s and did not climb above 40 percent until close to 1920. Consequently, when women were enfranchised in the western states, the denominator in the turnout index would not have doubled in value and, therefore, there would be less pressure on the turnout index to decline sharply. If this reasoning were true, then we would expect an additional artifact of the arithmetic to be a very slight or nonexistent increase in the value of the mobilization index, but an inspection of Table 6-3 shows that the mobilization indices in the western states increased as much as any other region of the country. This combination of no-change in turnout and a substantial increase in mobilization (the exact opposite of the pattern for the southern states) clearly suggests that women were more likely to vote in the west than they were anywhere else in the country.

These findings are not particularly surprising when one considers that this was the "women-suffrage" region of the country. With the exception of Kansas and New York, all the states where women were exercising full voting rights by 1918 were in this part of the country. In fact, only New Mexico, of all the western states did not extend full suffrage rights to women before 1920. Consequently, the emphasis placed on womens suffrage in this region of the country must have had a greater politicizing effect on women as they approached their first opportunity to vote. Alternatively, the fact that women were enfranchised so early in the West suggests that the dominant social motif of this region was not based on the belief that a woman's place was in the home. The exigencies of frontier life made it imperative that women participate both socially and economically in the life of the community. Therefore, when the same principle was extended to the political dimension, the role model for community involvement had already been established for women.

Pattern of Growth in
Personal Participation

What we have discussed thus far relates to the initial response by women upon being inducted into the electorate. We must now turn our attention to the years that followed and trace the pattern of growth by which women become increasingly more participatory, at least with respect to the ballot box. Unfortunately, given the problems of data collection mentioned earlier, we can not systematically trace the early stages of this growth process as Tingsten was able to do for the various western European nations he studied,[21] but undoubtedly the first substantial increment in female voting rates came about during the New Deal era. For one thing, women were being exposed to the same set of stimuli generated by the Smith-Roosevelt coalition, which mobilized large numbers of men into the political process. In addition, Chafe has noted that in many respects the Roosevelt administration had (consciously so) an added appeal for women.[22] The volume of domestic policy issues that confronted the president led him to consult with and to employ numerous women in his administration, including the first woman cabinet member; and throughout the administration, Eleanor Roosevelt continued her long-standing efforts designed to involve women in both governmental and Democratic party affairs.

While progress was made in mobilizing women voters during the Roosevelt years, the first tracings of post-World War II survey studies show that a significant difference between male and female participation rates still prevailed. As Table 6-4 indicates, the Survey Research Center's 1948 presidential election study showed that women's turnout was 13 percent behind the rate for men. Year by year, however, turnout for women increased bringing it closer to the rate for men, and as Table 6-5 demonstrates, the gap has now, for all practical purposes, disappeared. Although there is still a perceptible difference in the

Table 6-4

Sex Differences in Voting in Presidential Elections: 1948-1972

	1948	1952	1956	1960	1964	1968	1972
Male Turnout	69	72	80	80	73	76	76
Female Turnout	56	62	69	69	70	73	70
Percentage Point Differences (M-W)	13	10	11	11	3	3	6

Source: Center for Political Studies data in Marjorie Lansing, "The American Woman: Voter and Activist," in Jane S. Jaquette, ed., *Women in Politics* (New York: Wiley, 1974).

Table 6-5

Sex Differences in Voting in 1972 Presidential Election, National and Regional

	Nation	South	North & West
Male Turnout	64.1	57.3	67.1
Female Turnout	62.0	53.7	65.8
Percentage Point Differences	2.1	4.3	1.3

Source: U.S. Bureau of the Census, Current Population Report, "Population Characteristics," No. 253 (Washington, D.C.: U.S. Government Printing Office, 1973), table 1.

South, for the rest of the country and the nation as a whole the differences of 1.5-2 percent are negligible.

All the more interesting to look at are the differences in male-female voting rates by age group and by race. Table 6-6 is a reproduction of a table from Professor Marjorie Lansing's excellent summary of contemporary voting patterns of American women. The upper half of the table makes it clear that within the younger age cohorts women are just as likely to vote in presidential elections as are men and that this pattern has held true across the last three presidential elections. Two other aspects of these age differences are also interesting to note. A comparison of the older and younger age cohorts demonstrates the effects of the generational model, outlined earlier, which predicted that the gap in turnout rates for men and women would gradually close as women, exposed to the pre-1920 attitudes toward women in politics, grew older and left the population.

Secondly, by comparing the differences in voting by sex for the age cohorts below 65 years of age with those of the cohorts 65 and over, we can see eloquent support for the proposition that the New Deal had a substantial effect in mobilizing women to vote. While women, 65 and over, have generally voted at a rate 10 percent or more below males of the same age group during the last three elections, women below 65 have for the most part been very close or equal

Table 6-6

Sex Differences in Presidential Voting, by Age Group: 1964, 1968, and 1972

	1964		1968		1972	
Age Groups	Male	Female	Male	Female	Male	Female
18 to 24 yr					48	49
21 to 24 yr	53	52	53	53	50	52
25 to 29 yr					58	58
30 to 34 yr	66	65	63	63	66	67
35 to 44 yr	75	72	74	72	66	67
45 to 54 yr	79	75	78	76	72	70
55 to 64 yr	80	74	79	74	72	69
65 to 74 yr	78	67	79	69	73	64
75 yr and up	67	50	68	51	67	49

Source: Adapted from Marjorie Lansing, "The American Woman: Voter and Activist," in Jane S. Jaquette, ed., *Women in Politics* (New York: Wiley, 1974), table 1-4.

to men of their same age cohorts in their voting rates. Since women in the age cohorts, 45-54 and 55-64, were coming of age during the 1930s and 1940s it seems clear that the stimulus of the Smith-Roosevelt campaign coalition had a substantial impact in leading these women to higher levels of voting participation than was characteristic of women who came of age during the twenties or earlier.

With respect to race, Table 6-7 shows the turnout rates, by age group, for the total population and then for blacks and whites separately. We can see that black women are less likely to vote than white women even in the younger age cohorts, a clear indication that the extension of suffrage rights to women in the late nineteenth and early twentieth centuries was, for all intents and purposes, an extension of suffrage rights to white women. What is worth noting, however, is that younger and middle-aged black women equal or exceed the participation of black men in the same age groupings. In a recent discussion of the voting patterns of American black women, Lansing has shown that this tendency for black women to vote at higher rates than black men is true only in certain age groups, but that it also shows up in certain educational and occupational strata as well. She goes on to argue that the rate of participation among black women is likely to increase in the coming years.[23]

To summarize, we have seen that large numbers of white women refrained from voting when they first received their full suffrage rights during the period from 1890 to 1920, while for black women, the adoption of the 19th Amendment was by and large irrelevant. In the intervening years the participation rate of white women increased steadily, helped along substantially by the politicizing effects of the New Deal era. Black women, however, did not begin to participate in substantial numbers until the passage of the 1965 Voting Rights

Table 6-7

Sex Differences in Voting in 1972 Presidential Election, by Age Grouping and Race

Age Groups	Total Population		White		Black	
	Male	Female	Male	Female	Male	Female
18 to 20	47.7	48.8	51.0	51.0	25.6	35.2
21 to 24	49.7	51.7	51.2	53.8	38.4	38.0
25 to 29	57.6	58.9	58.8	59.5	50.1	49.8
30 to 34	62.1	61.7	63.1	63.2	56.1	54.3
35 to 44	65.9	66.7	67.2	68.0	57.8	60.8
45 to 54	72.0	69.9	73.1	71.1	62.6	61.8
55 to 64	72.4	69.2	73.4	70.2	62.1	61.1
65 to 74	73.2	64.3	74.8	65.3	59.8	53.9
75 and up	65.9	49.1	67.7	50.6	49.4	32.5

Source: U.S. Bureau of the Census, Current Population Reports (Washington, D.C.: U.S. Government Printing Office, 1973), table 1.

Act and, consequently, their voting rate still lags behind that of white women. Overall, by the 1972 presidential election, the differences between male and female voting rates in national elections had virtually disappeared. The question that remains is what have been the politicizing effects of this voting history on women in the American political system?

**The Political Effects of
Voting Rights**

In order to understand the politicizing effects voting had on American women it will be necessary for us to consider the systemic context within which women struggled for, achieved, and then began to exercise their right to vote. What we have come to call the woman suffrage movement first began in earnest in the 1840s, and its objectives regarding the status of women in society were quite revolutionary for the times.[24] The feminists of the mid-nineteenth century wrote and spoke about the need for economic, social, and sexual (particularly relating to child-rearing) as well as political reforms. In short, they were calling for complete equality for all women in society. However, it should be noted that already a wedge was being driven between black and white on the question of political reforms. In an action that was to foreshadow a similar movement by the southern states a half century later, most northern states during the period prior to the Civil War adopted restrictions against voting by free-colored.[25]

The controversy over abolition, the Civil War, and the sectional conflict which marked the decade and a half after the war, all served to delay serious consideration and response to the feminists' proposals, and, as the debate over women's rights dragged on, a new generation of feminists came forward around the turn of the century. This group of women seemed more disposed to compromise and to accept a change in the laws relating solely to voting rights rather than the broader sweep of reform proposals put forward in preceding years.

In consequence, victory for women was finally sealed in the passage of the 19th Amendment to the U.S. Constitution. However, in the aftermath of this achievement there was a sense of loss and defeat. For a brief while, there had been some discussion about the desirability of organizing a woman's political party to carry on the fight for women's rights, but the disappointing perform- ance by women as voters in the wake of their enfranchisement quickly vitiated this possibility. Furthermore, the poor voting record of women led many male leaders of the two established parties to question the need for them to offer serious legislative responses to the various reform proposals being pushed by women's groups. As a result, the League of Women Voters, a nonpartisan and nonoffice-seeking group, soon became the dominant voice for women in politics in the United States, calling upon women to focus on those issues that were of unique concern to them—social welfare and education.[26]

Two other developments subsequently strengthened this regressive trend moving women away from the central arena of professional politics. As we noted earlier, the Roosevelts, both Franklin and Eleanor, gave the political status of women a boost during the thirties, but, as it happened, this boost only served to reify further the principle of women concentrating on "women's issues." Most of the women who came to positions of prominence in the administration or in the Democratic Party brought with them the perspectives of social workers or educators, which is exactly what so many of them were. As Chafe has pointed out, there were no women placed in charge of the major boards, commissions, and agencies that directed our nation's war effort in the forties, nor were women to be found in the decision-making councils that planned the conversion back to a peace-time economy in this country or the political and economic revitaliza- tion of western Europe and Japan.[27]

A second factor enhancing the isolation of women from professional political roles was the development of *volunteerism* in our society, a process symbolized by the growth of the League of Women Voters. The term *volunteerism* is actually somewhat misleading. The point that is at issue is not the fact that women volunteer their free time to participate in some organized activity; some men engage in volunteer activities as well. The question is what is the form and the content of the activities that are undertaken. There are clearly significant differences between participation in the Council on Foreign Relations and joining the local hospital auxiliary.

The National Organization for Women has provided a cogent description of what these differences are in their distinction between "service-oriented" and "political or change-oriented" volunteering.[28] Service-oriented volunteer activities are those that are person or situation directed, as opposed to change-oriented volunteering, which is directed toward inducing change in the broader social, political, or economic system. It is "service-oriented" volunteering that became the unique province of women, especially white women, because, as many persons argued, it was the type of work that would otherwise not get done.

As for black women, many of them could not afford to engage in volunteer activities, not because they were staying at home, but because their circumstances forced them to seek employment. There were others, however, who did engage in service-oriented volunteer activities, but they did so with a twist. They undertook these activities because they felt that the white society would not, through its governmental agencies, respond to the legitimate needs of black people for social services. Once they perceived that the government was prepared to respond, their efforts swiftly turned to change-oriented goals and active protest against the broader system. As a result, the government assumed the responsibility of supporting many of the activities blacks had previously had to support out of their own volunteer resources.

So once again we see differences in the political experiences of black and white women, differences that, it can be argued, have had important consequences in their politicizing effects on American women. Obviously, the steady growth in voting participation on the part of white women has not led to significant levels of participation by these persons in professional political roles. On the other hand, black women, who only recently have begun to vote in larger numbers, are participating in professional political roles in roughly the same proportion as white women. Clearly it would seem that the politicizing effects of their involvement in the protest movement and in efforts to extract a larger share of benefits from the political system have more than made up for their lack of experience in the traditional act of voting.

What will be the pattern of women's involvement in professional political roles in the coming decades? It is worth noting that many white women (e.g., the mother of South Boston) have come to embrace nontraditional means of political involvement in order to induce change in the system, but this phenomenon has remained relatively limited, focused on the issue of busing in northern, urban school districts. It would seem that more and different types of politicizing experiences will not be sufficient to move women across the threshold to rapid advancement in professional politics. What is now required will be a focus on the question of private economic roles.

As we noted earlier the feminists of a century and a quarter ago viewed the progress of women's rights as whole cloth. They did not see that political equality could be sustained in the absence of economic and social equality. In this light, the achievement of equal voting rights without equal standing in economics could be viewed as an artificial concession by men in our society. What is needed is the fundamental achievement of equality in career and income opportunities. While black women have long since established themselves in economic roles, their occupational and income horizons have been severely limited. As for most white women, particularly middle-class white women, they have hardly begun to establish an economic identity separate from but equal to that of their husbands.[29] Until women compete with men for economic roles within the system and thereby come to view politics, as men do—one of several career alternatives—it is difficult to envision them competing equally with men for professional roles in the political arena.

Notes

1. Wilma R. Krause, "Political Implications of Gender Roles: A Review of the Literature," *American Political Science Review* 68 (December, 1974), pp. 1706-1723.

2. Irene L. Murphy, *Public Policy and the Status of Women* (Boston: Lexington/Heath, 1974).

3. Krause, op. cit.

4. Some examples of the literature that have dealt with this subject are Lester Milbrath, *Political Participation* (Chicago: Rand McNally, 1965); Gabrid Almond and Sidney Verba, *The Civic Culture* (Princeton: Princeton University Press, 1963); Sidney Verba and Norman H. Nie, *Participation in America* (New York: Harper & Row, 1972).

5. Jerrold G. Rusk and John J. Stucker, "An Historical Review of Suffrage Legislation in the United States," in W.D. Burnham, et al., eds., *Behavioral Guide to the Study of American Electoral History* (Cambridge: MIT Press, forthcoming).

6. John S. Mill, "The Subjection of Women," in Alice S. Rossi, ed., *Essays on Sex Equality* (Chicago: University of Chicago Press, 1970).

7. Charles Seymour and Donald P. Frary *How the World Votes*, 2 vols. (Springfield: Nichols, 1918).

8. Mildred Adams et al., *Victory: How Women Won It* (New York: H.W. Wilson, 1940).

9. William H. Chafe, *The American Woman; Her Changing Social, Economic and Political Roles, 1920-1970* (New York: Oxford University Press, 1972).

10. Among the writers who have addressed this topic are: W.D. Burnham, *Critical Elections and the Mainsprings of American Politics* (New York: Norton, 1970); Richard J. Jensen, *The Winning of the Midwest: Social and Political Conflict, 1888-1896* (Chicago: University of Chicago Press, 1971); Paul J. Kleppner, *The Cross of Culture: A Social Analysis of Midwestern Politics, 1850-1900* (Riverside, N.J.: Free Press, 1970).

11. John J. Stucker, *The Impact of Woman Suffrage on Patterns of Voter Participation in the United States; Quasi-Experimental and Real-Time Analyses, 1890-1920* (Ph.D. Dissertation, University of Michigan, 1973).

12. U.S. Senate, Committee on Woman Suffrage, Hearing before 63rd Congress, 1st Session, Washington, 1913.

13. Herbert Tingsten, *Political Behavior* (London: King, 1937).

14. Chafe, op. cit.

15. Stucker, op. cit.

16. Harold F. Gosnell, *Why Europe Votes* (Chicago: University of Chicago Press, 1930).

17. V.O. Key, Jr., *Southern Politics* (New York: Knopf, 1949).

18. Jerrold G. Rusk and John J. Stucker, "The Effect of the Southern System of Elections Laws on Voter Participation: A Reply to V.O. Key," in Joel Silbey, et al., eds., *The History of Popular Voting Behavior in the U.S.* (Princeton: Princeton University Press, forthcoming).

19. William A. McPhee and Robert A. Smith, "A Model for Analyzing Voting Systems," in William McPhee and William A. Glaser, eds., *Public Opinion and Congressional Elections* (Riverside, N.J.: Free Press, 1962).

20. Charles E. Merriam and Harold G. Gosnell, *Non-Voting: Causes and Methods of Control* (Chicago: University of Chicago Press, 1924).

21. Tingsten, op. cit.

22. Chafe, op. cit.

23. Marjorie Lansing, "The Voting Patterns of American Black Women," a paper presented at the 1973 Annual Meeting of the American Political Science Association, New Orleans, Louisiana, September 4-8, 1973.

24. Adams, op. cit; Chafe, op. cit.

25. Rusk and Stucker, "An Historical Review," op. cit.

26. Chafe, op. cit.

27. Ibid.

28. National Organization for Women, Report of the NOW Task Force on Volunteerism, Washington, D.C., November 1973.

29. Judith Stiehm and Ruth Scott, "Female and Male: Voluntary and Chosen Participation Sex, SES, and Participation," a paper presented at the 1974 Annual Meeting of the American Political Science Association, Chicago, Illinois, August 29-September 2, 1974.

7

Government Policy and the Legal Status of Women

Roxanne Barton Conlin

The initial problem is ascertaining what the government's policy toward women is. We will attempt to explore, superficially, three areas concerning the legal status of women: employment, education, and marriage.

In 1963, Congress passed the Equal Pay Act, followed by passage of the Equal Employment Opportunity Act in 1964. The act was originally proposed to eliminate race discrimination. The amendment to prohibit sex discrimination was offered by a congressman known to be adamantly opposed to the bill. The tactic was to attach this amendment in order to prevent final passage of the bill. This man apparently thought that requiring employers to treat men and women equally was so ludicrous that his colleagues would be unable to support the entire act if his amendment was adopted. Fortunately, his tactic misfired and Title 7 became the law of the land. The first Equal Employment Opportunity Commissioners openly expressed reservations about enforcement of the sex provisions and, in fact, one commissioner ridiculed the concept and assured employers that it would be ignored. Congress did not give the Equal Employment Opportunity Commission direct enforcement powers, or "cease and desist" powers, but, in what was perceived as a compromise, left enforcement to the Federal Courts. A few individual women, bolstered by feminist organizations, undertook to assure that the sex discrimination provisions would be enforced and, because the law allowed access to the courts, they were able to begin the arduous process of establishing precedent on a case-by-case basis.

One of the most serious difficulties were the so-called "protective" laws—state laws that prohibited women from working in certain occupations, lifting more than a certain weight, or working more than a certain number of hours. Initially, the Equal Employment Opportunity Commission declined to state that those laws were unconstitutional. In 1969, four years after the effective date of the act, the Equal Employment Opportunity Commission ruled that these restrictive laws were unconstitutional insofar as they applied to covered employers. The courts have agreed without exception.

Additionally, all but nine states have passed laws prohibiting discrimination on the basis of sex in employment. Most state enforcement agencies have "cease and desist" powers.

It is the clearly stated and enforceable public policy of this nation that employment discrimination on the basis of sex is unlawful.

115

Or is it? As of 1971, every state but Delaware had at least one law restricting women's rights to compete equally for employment. As of today, only sixteen states have repealed those laws or extended them to cover men and it appears that the courts consider the existence of those laws a defense to a claim for backpay. The agencies that are expected to enforce the states' public policy are hampered by inadequate funding and understaffing. The Equal Employment Opportunity Commission has 100,000 cases pending. The administrative process intended to provide a speedy remedy has become instead a roadblock to enforcement. Under federal law, a complainant must wait nearly a year before filing in court. Under most state laws, the existence of an administrative remedy prevents any court action until the administrative remedy is exhausted.

In view of these contradictions, it is not surprising that the statistics fail to reflect gains on the part of women workers. Of all women in this country, 54.2 percent work. Women earn three dollars for every five dollars earned by a man in the same occupation and the gap has been steadily increasing since 1955. In 1974, female chemical engineering graduates earned $833 per month, while male colleagues earned $928. Women math majors earned thirty dollars less per month than their male counterparts; accounting majors fifty-two dollars less per month. The median income of male high-school dropouts is $8,945 per year. Women college graduates earn $9,062, an average of $117 per year more. Male college graduates have a median income of $14,351.

Individual people within and without enforcement agencies are struggling mightily to overcome the obstacles to fair employment. There are notable successes. The AT&T settlement was the most publicized, but additional millions in back pay have been recovered under federal and state law that, because of confidentiality provisions, have never been made public. Women as a class are, however, still confined to underpaid, underutilized positions, public policy notwithstanding.

Part of the problem of fair employment results from unequal education opportunities. The rigid sex roles assigned to men and women in our society are enforced on children by the public schools. The school system has in the past and still continues to neglect the full development of young women. Instead educators prepare them only to assume the role designated for female adults— full-time homemakers. Female children are subject to different standards and regulations than are male children. Many schools do not permit young women the same opportunity to develop skills in areas considered "for boys only." For example, girls are not encouraged to develop physical strength. Textbooks and other curricular material ignore or denigrate women and girls. Although this type of conditioning has been recognized as unfair and discriminatory when applied to minorities, the application of the same kind of conditioning to women is seen as an acceptable form of preparation as young girls learn to assume a "woman's" role as an adult.[1]

With rare exception, the public school districts in the United States provide a markedly different education for male and female students. Some courts, the U.S. Congress and the state legislatures, have reacted positively with efforts to equalize education for students of both sexes. For example, Congress passed Title IX of the Education Amendments, to be effective July, 1972. Title IX was written to prohibit sex discrimination in any educational program receiving federal funds. It applies to virtually all of the public school systems in the country in addition to approximately 2,500 private colleges and universities receiving federal funds. Worthy as Title IX is, however, it has some serious flaws, both legal and practical. Title IX provides for no private right of action for those suffering from discriminatory treatment. Also, HEW, the enforcing agency, seems to have an apparent lack of interest in this since it failed to issue proposed regulations until more than two years after the effective date of the act.[2]

Perhaps women should be grateful for the delay. Reports circulating indicate that the final regulations now on the President's desk are woefully inadequate. They do not prohibit discrimination in textbooks or curricular material. They do not even require an examination of those materials for bias nor do they require any attempt to counteract the narrow portrayal of women. They do not require equal expenditure of funds for male and female students in athletics. A new provision exempts all contact sports even where the single sex team is the only team. Schools aren't required to start a female team. One of the most damaging provisions was not even mentioned in the proposed regulations. It requires that each school set up its own grievance procedure. HEW will defer any action on a complaint until the grievance procedure is completed. There is no time limit and there are no minimum standards for the procedure. HEW has, in effect, turned its enforcement powers over to the institutions charged with violating the law. It doesn't seem very promising.

Another avenue for enforcement is of course the courts. Many cases have eliminated discriminatory admission policies, sex-segregated courses, and discrimination in athletics. However, because there is no strong enforceable national public policy, some courts have not felt compelled to allow women an equal educational opportunity. A lower court judge, in a case involving a young girl who wished to compete with boys in a noncontact sport said:

The present generation of our younger male population has not become so decadent that boys will experience a thrill in defeating girls in running contests, whether the girls be members of their own team or an adversary team. It could well be that many boys would feel compelled to forego entering track events if they were required to compete with girls on their own teams or adversary teams. With boys vying with girls . . . the challenge to win, and the glory of achievement, at least for many boys would lose incentive and become nullified. Athletic competition builds character in our boys. We do not need that kind of character in our girls.[3]

Other courts, perhaps more enlightened, have concluded that prohibiting female athletes from participation with boys in such noncontact sports as tennis, golf, track, and skiing violates the 14th Amendment.[4]

Another grave difficulty is that of filtering a national policy down to those who have day-to-day contact with students. In order to convince recalcitrant school boards and administrators, it is necessary that a policy be not only stated, but also that it be vigorously enforced. In the case of education, that seems unlikely to happen.

The last area, marriage, is the most difficult because policy is generally established on a state rather than a national level. The prevailing social structure requires every adult to choose a semipermanent partner for social and sexual purposes, formalizing these partnerships by marriage. The state, however, becomes a third party in marriages because it imposes obligations, divides responsibilities, and restricts the activities of married persons on the basis of their sex. Our laws governing the marriage structure are replete with an archaic bias towards the traditional role of men and women, assigning roles to persons on the basis of their sex rather than on the basis of individual differences. Statutory and case law, in most states, affirms what are considered traditional male and female patterns of behavior, thus steering women into the fully supported role of full-time homemakers and men into the role of year-round full-time breadwinners. Please note that the recent movement toward equality between the sexes does not preclude this traditional interpersonal structure; true equality will result in tangible benefits for women who choose to perform homemaking services.[5]

Georgia is one of the states that is most open about the underlying concepts of female inferiority. In its 1974 statute it declares:

The husband is head of the family and the wife is subject to him, her legal existence is merged in the husband's, except so far as the law recognizes her separately, either for her own protection or for her benefit, or for the preservation of the public order.[6]

Among the rights that are different for married women are certain aspects of important property rights. Married women are statutorily perceived as fiscally irresponsible, weak, and childish creatures for whom unusual precautions must be taken. In Alabama, for example, women are not allowed to purchase land without their husband's written permission; and in Kentucky, married women may not convey their own separately held real property without their husband's consent. The presumption is that in Alabama and Kentucky all women are less knowledgeable than all men about real estate transactions.[7]

Another right that is affected radically by sex and marital status is the legal concept of domicile. A domicile is defined as the place where a person has a settled connection for certain legal purposes, either because the person's home is there or because the law assigns it. Domicile determines jurisdiction and venue in divorce, probate, and guardianship proceedings as well as the place where individuals may vote or seek public office, receive public assistance, or attend state-supported universities. Domicile also determines where an individual will serve on juries and pay taxes. In many states, the domicile of a married woman is the domicile of the husband, regardless of where she actually resides. All of the benefits and privileges of domicile for a married woman are thus determined by her marital status. However obsolete, the legal duty of the wife to follow and live with her husband wherever he goes remains alive and well.[8]

In several states contracts for services between husband and wife are considered invalid by the strictures of public policy. Alabama does permit husbands and wives to make such contracts, allowing, however, a rebuttable statutory presumption that the husband is dominant.[9] These provisions are thought by some to protect women.

Women may suffer in strange ways from their husband's irresponsible behavior. Only recently did the U.S. Supreme Court strike down an Arizona statute that revoked a woman's license to operate a motor vehicle if her husband failed to pay a judgment debt for negligent driving.[10]

Another statutory embarrassment is the "feme sole trader" statute. In Pennsylvania a woman may become a "feme sole trader," or a female entitled to conduct her own business, merely by petitioning the court and providing two witnesses. Florida recently repealed a statute requiring a woman to prove her "character, habits, education, and mental capacity for business" to do business in precisely the same manner as any man who undergoes no such tests to go into business. Males are, under the law and by gender alone, competent in the business world. The women of Pennsylvania should be considered fortunate, however, since their legislature has specifically provided that a woman may purchase a sewing machine without her husband's consent.[11]

New Mexico provides an example of the literal reality that for some "husband and wife are one." In that state a woman who works for the same public agency as her husband is not paid directly for her labor. Instead the agency insists on issuing *her* paychecks to her husband in *his* name. Not surprisingly, she has filed suit.[12]

What links these cases together is the common law "chattel" status of married women. While this status may have once had its uses, today it only emphasizes the failure of the law to recognize women as full and independent human beings.[13]

Many women feel that it is their option to remain at home as full-time unpaid laborers. Indeed there is a widespread belief that under these circumstances a woman is entitled to rely on her husband to support her. The facts, however, are different.

In the courts a woman who lives with her husband has no financial protection since the courts have steadfastly refused to interfere with an ongoing relationship to assure the wife her "right to support."[14]

The most prominent case here is *Maguire vs. Maguire.* The husband was an affluent but stingy farmer who refused to provide his wife of thirty-four years with even necessities, despite the fact that the wife had participated on an almost equal basis with her husband in operating the farm. For the last three or four years, the husband had given his wife no money, nor had he provided her with any clothing except a coat. She was also not allowed to have any charge accounts. Their house had no bathroom, no bathing facilities, and no sink—water had to be pumped from an outdoor well. The furnace could not provide sufficient warmth and the furniture was shabby. The car was twenty-four-years old and did not have a working heater. The district court ordered the husband to pay to improve and repair the house, which meant installing plumbing and purchasing better furniture, appliances, and a better source of transportation. A fifty dollar per month allowance to the wife was also ordered. The Supreme Court reversed the decision saying:

As long as the home is maintained and the parties are living as husband and wife it may be said that the husband is legally supporting his wife and the purpose of the marriage relation is being carried out. Public policy requires such a holding.[15]

Rather than protecting homemakers, the net effect of the existing case law and inconsistent statutes is that a homemaker must rely on her husband's benevolence. Women pay an exorbitant price for their so-called right to support. As a class, women have been denied equal opportunity in employment and education because it is assumed erroneously that these opportunities are not needed so long as they are being "supported."[16]

Taxation indirectly states public policy and the effect of those laws on a homemaking spouse is infrequently considered when legislation is proposed. The Iowa legislature recently rectified a hidden discrimination in the taxation of jointly held property to a surviving widow. The interpretation worked to the detriment of an estimated 2,400 to 3,600 women every year.

In the income tax area discrimination results generally from the taxation of two wage-earner families, resulting in unfair treatment of families wherein the wife chooses to work for pay.

The entire tax system rests squarely on the breadwinner-homemaker dichotomy. It disadvantages persons of both sexes who fail to fit the stereotypes. It does not even treat women who are homemakers fairly because it denies the economic value of their work and assumes by law that someone is caring for their economic needs.

There is no coherent, consistent enforceable public policy that requires women and men be treated equally under the law.

Where should women look for the formulation of such a policy? To the United States Supreme Court? It is certainly moving toward an interpretation of the 14th Amendment that would include equal protection of the laws for women citizens. But the standards it is applying are virtually incomprehensible. The lower courts are faced with increasingly more difficult issues and fluctuating legal principles on which to base their decisions.

Maybe Congress? Congress did pass the Equal Rights Amendment and send it to the states. However, there are more than 800 federal laws that discriminate on the basis of sex. Military academies, social security, and numerous other areas remain untouched.

State legislatures? Some are changing and modifying their laws and some are not. The states wherein the need is greatest are the slowest to react. The Executive branch? Surely not. The bureaucracy impedes the progress of women. Several examples have been given you.

We must look to ourselves and other women. Women are, after all, one-half of the public. It is unfortunate that women are not one-half of the public policy makers, but, if we are successful at organizing in our own enlightened self-interest, we can change that.

It is a slow and painful process—we must not lose patience. On the other hand, women cannot be expected to wait quietly for judges and legislators to mete out one right at a time. We must understand the seriousness of the issues confronting us. This society is in the midst of a social revolution because the idea of full social legal and economic equality for women is indeed revolutionary.

Notes

1. Roxanne Barton Conlin, "Equal Protection Versus Equal Rights Amendment—Where Are We Now?" *Drake Law Review* 24 (Winter, 1975), pp. 322-323.

2. Ibid., p. 323.

3. Ibid., p. 325. Reprinted with permission of the *Drake Law Review*.

4. Ibid.

5. Ibid., p. 269.

6. Georgia Code Ann. 53-501, 1974.

7. Conlin, op. cit., p. 270.

8. Ibid., pp. 270-1.

9. Ibid., p. 271.

10. Ibid.

11. Ibid.

12. Ibid., p. 272.

13. Ibid.

14. Ibid., p. 275.

15. Ibid., pp. 277-8. Reprinted with permission of the *Drake Law Review*.

16. Ibid.

8

Alternatives for Social Change: The Future Status of Women

Carolyn Shaw Bell

The future status of women will, of course, evolve from the present status of women. Nevertheless, it will not unfold as an inevitable progression or even be predictable. The seeds of the future may lie within the present, but not all the seeds will find fertile soil and some that take root will wither and some will be cut down. A researcher, fifty years from now, who reviews these papers may, possibly, be struck by the prescience with which the contributors dealt with issues that will have long since become familiar to that researcher's accepted world. But then again, perhaps such a researcher grubbing about in archives will find this material not even worth a footnote, since it so clearly missed all the right directions to history. The future status of women cannot be predicted from our present position because it will require social action, which means choosing goals and programs to reach these goals.

To discern the outlines of any future in what the present offers means accepting any offer with a commitment to push for social change.[1] In a real sense, therefore, the future status of women depends on what goals we are willing to work for and what programs we will support. On the basis of what we learn about our present situation we can dream about the future, but to turn fantasy into reality we must construct a strategy for change—we must choose among alternatives for social action.

Our situation today can best be described as a society trying to assimilate a revolution. The revolution that has occurred has shattered conventional assumptions about the status of women. It is no longer possible to feel comfortable with the assertion that a woman's chief occupation is that of a homemaker, that her role is that of dependent daughter or wife or widow. It is simply unrealistic to define women in terms of marriage and the family without recognizing the individual woman as an independent person with legal rights, economic resources, and responsibilities to herself, as well as to others. The revolution has occurred before the passage of the Equal Rights Amendment, with an assault on the existing structure of society by changes in laws and court decisions, a reshaping of the economy from shifts in relative prices and economic output, and irreversible changes in the culture—in response to all of the facets of the women's movement. The revolution in the status of women can most simply be summarized in the fact that thirty-two million working women won't go home again.

They went home at the end of World War II, when the vast increase in women's employment quickly dwindled, because jobs were needed for returning veterans and women were needed to care for their families. They went home in the great depression of the thirties, when women were dismissed from their jobs or denied employment because men needed the work. Such reasoning is simply unacceptable today. The revolution freeing women from their automatic classification as housewives has taken place. Not that it has been completed—the mopping-up operations will last at least another generation. But what then? To envision the future status of women means seeing more than labor-market projections—it means seeing wider opportunities for women as well as new opportunities for employment.

An alternative goal exists in another revolution, one just beginning to take shape—not in terms of the rights of women but of the responsibilities of human beings. This revolution involves family formation and the upbringing of children, marriage and divorce, and the process of human growth and development. However, to an economist, the revolution affects nothing more than the well-known phenomenon of specialization and the division of labor.

In every culture that we know, men's jobs and women's jobs have always existed although the specific chores that fall to men and women differ throughout the world and over time. For almost one hundred years in this country and in the industrialized West the woman's place has been in the home. When she has gone out to sell her labor, the jobs available to her in the economy have been, unlike men's jobs, low-paying, low-skilled, and dead-end. These are the conditions today's revolution is changing—the traditional division of labor in the marketplace can no longer be taken for granted.[2]

One result, for men, has been to relieve some of the crushing burden of responsibility they have traditionally been assigned. Men no longer need to be the sole support of a wife and family. When women seize new opportunities for education and employment, they acquire greater abilities to earn income and can share the financial responsibility that was formerly exclusively male.[3] However, the responsibilities that women have borne—of caring for home and family—have not yet been shifted or relieved. The rest of our culture's division of labor—the jobs at home—remains untouched. The task of the next revolution is to bring about a situation where the work performed at home is a responsibility for human beings instead of a burden for women.

The new division of labor within the marketplace has not, of course, done away with men's jobs and women's jobs. Severe differentials persist between men's and women's earnings. Occupational segregation has surfaced as a phenomenon of great significance. Like many other topics that first emerged in analyzing the status of women, occupational segregation has major implications for both sexes, it is not very well understood, and it calls for interdisciplinary analysis.[4]

Any comparative analysis of the jobs held over the past fifty years shows that occupational segregation has changed very little, overall. While it is true that sex stereotyping has declined in the sense that women have penetrated the traditionally male trades and professions, sex-typing of occupations remains, and most women continue to be concentrated in very few types of work, labelled "women's jobs" because few men are employed.[5] Such occupational segregation will not change much, in the future, until the next revolution gains momentum.[6] Segregation on the job, and the automatic relegation of women to positions as secretaries, assistants, and technical aides can largely be traced to occupational segregation within the home. Only change in the division of labor within the home will allow men and women to compete equally for jobs outside the home.

Much of the work done by economists analyzing the labor market bears on this hypothesis. Occupational segregation has emerged as a major topic for investigation in the search to isolate the forces of discrimination. Perhaps the greatest contribution of economics to any analysis of women's status is the work of Gary Becker, Kenneth Arrow, Barbara Bergmann, and others, which makes us very chary of using the word "discrimination."[7] Inequalities in income or earnings, unequal opportunities, disproportionate representation of two groups, and disparate amounts of resources devoted to two groups—none of these necessarily illustrate discrimination. Obviously, for example, average earnings of skilled workers exceed those of unskilled workers not because of discrimination but because of differences in productivity that yield different returns in the market. In labor market analysis, economists have found it helpful to restrict the term "discrimination" to that proportion of any differential in wages, employment, or conditions of work that cannot be attributed to economic phenomena.[8] So the close scrutiny of all differences between men and women in the labor market has provided considerable evidence suggesting that occupational segregation in the market is linked not to discrimination, but to the division of labor at home.

There is, first, the analysis of the supply of labor, by women, as a function of their home responsibilities.[9] Many so-called "women's jobs" are also part-time or seasonal jobs. As such they are particularly appropriate for women—they can work while their children are in school or when they can conveniently be away from home. Women use different criteria in job search and job selection than the criteria used by men. They not only look for working hours that will mesh with their children's schoolday or their husband's workshift, but they take jobs to minimize their travel time or to allow them to go shopping on the way home, and they avoid jobs requiring Saturday assignments or overtime work, because that would prevent them from being home with the rest of the family. Since not all occupations meet the characteristics sought by women, those that do have a large supply of women applicants for the jobs available. As one result, wages may fall below those of another occupation where the supply of workers is less. As another result, women may heavily outnumber men, who are willing to supply their labor in other markets.

According to this interpretation, occupational segregation does not reflect any overt or covert discrimination, but the preferences of the women themselves—their decision to apply for some jobs, but not others. The differential in earnings that results is compensated for, in part, by what economists call "psychic income," that is the nonmonetary satisfactions provided by the job's location, hours of work, or flexibility.

Another analysis of the division of labor in the market shows that the quality of labor services offered by women differs from that supplied by men, and this, too, traces to the division of labor at home. One such qualitative difference is experience: women spend fewer years, or fewer continuous years, in the labor force than do men.[10] They leave their jobs when their husbands move or to have children. As a result, they lack the long-term work involvement that leads to acquired skills, familiarity with routine, confidence in dealing with the unexpected, and acquaintance with others in the field and with accepted and developing ways of doing business. They may actually lose what skills they started with, if trade practices or jargon, technical methods, or professional procedures have shifted markedly during the time they were away from employment. Women are, simply, not worth as much as the more experienced male workers. Their responsibilities at home mean that the quality of their labor supply in the market falls short.

This argument, of course, attributes the differential in earnings between men and women to that part of payment that is the return to experience or to the skills gained on the job. A simple comparison of work histories of men and women can demonstrate the difference in levels of experience and, hence, in earnings. The argument can also be used to explain some part of occupational segregation.

Men's jobs and women's jobs exist partly because occupations differ in the length and amount of experience required to fill a given position. The relegation of women to assistants, aides, or secretaries rather than their advancement to managers, account executives, or department heads represents not discrimination, but sound economic behavior. Women who move in and out of the labor force are not good material for on-the-job training or promotion, or even for informal grooming by encouragement and advice for whatever higher positions might open up. Employers invest in special courses or job rotation for their employees because they expect a payoff in the future when these employees can do more or do it better. Therefore, they cannot invest in a woman, who may give unexpected notice when the family moves or who quits when a new family member arrives. Because women lack the necessary employment experience, qualified women for many occupations do not exist and certainly number far fewer than men. Occupational segregation frequently results from differences in lifetime work patterns between men and women and, indirectly, from the existence of women's home responsibilities.

Now, all these situations—the fact that the job market offers a limited number of employment opportunities that mesh with women's work at home, and that women exhibit, to use the analyst's jargon, a lesser attachment to the labor force than do men—cannot be dismissed. We have not reviewed this evidence to dispute it. But the way in which these situations are viewed and reported deserves close attention. It is the interpretation of this evidence that we wish to question.

A great deal of writing in this area refers to women's preferences or to women's options. These terms, especially in the context in which they are used, imply voluntary action on the part of women, deliberate choice among alternatives, and decisions individually and probably rationally made. Thus, it is said, the situations just described, where women's jobs and work histories fit their patterns of home responsibilities, exist because that is what women want. Those who see the employment behavior of women in this way, rely, logically enough, upon the basic economic model of decision-making for the individual entering the labor market or supplying labor services.

This model says that we all have limited amounts of time and we can all think of alternative uses for this time.[11] Among them are employment, work at home, recreation, taking care of children, sheer idleness, personal care, education, and volunteer work. Each has its rewards and each its costs, for if we do one thing we give up the time we might have spent doing something else. So we choose to allocate our total time among these various activities. Since time belongs to each of us, the economic model assumes that each of us chooses so as to maximize his or her individual satisfaction. But we question whether this model, which, by the way, has been most elaborately developed by men, can be straightforwardly applied to both men and women without some further thinking. It implies a condition of freedom for the individual that probably doesn't exist anywhere. None of us are free from the constraints of our society and the obligations we feel to others. However, we suggest that, given our society, the constraints and obligations we feel probably differ between men and women. Unfortunately, little discussion exists on the nature of decision-making, as between the sexes, nor is there much analysis of the parameters of women's freedom to choose.[12]

Paradoxically enough, another whole body of writing refers to constraints on women's choices and to the necessity for them to care for home and family. This implies a total lack of freedom. In this view women face no decisions about how to allocate their time because the outcome has already been determined by social and cultural mores. The very term, *women's home responsibilities*, makes the point, as does every analysis of women's careers in terms of conflict.[13] We believe that this interpretation is more accurate or, perhaps, more realistic than the economist's model in analyzing the options for women. Most people take it for granted that women have only limited choices—this assumption is reiterated daily in common speech. A few examples, anecdotal though they may be, will illustrate.

A young woman graduated from college three years ago and works as a research assistant at the university where her husband is completing his Ph.D. She says, "Right now, while I have to work, I couldn't manage studying at night. Jerry helps some, but with his job and his evening classes he doesn't have much time so there's a lot for me to do at home, and graduate school will have to wait." Another remark comes from the mother of a four-year-old. Discussing her decision not to push for a managerial job despite her ten years' experience in the field, she says, "Since Tom and I want to have another child I won't be able to work full-time." One more—a woman Ph.D. explaining why this degree came fifteen years after her bachelor's degree—says, "Of course I tried to keep up with the literature, but it was impossible to continue my research when I had to go to Texas." What was in Texas? Her medical doctor husband interned and did his specialty at a hospital there.

What is significant are the verbs these women use—"I *want* to have another child." That speaks of exercising her own will. However, the other verbs are different: "I *had* to go to Texas." "I *won't be able to* work full-time." "School will *have* to wait." These do not sound like decisions freely taken. If one listens to women talking about their market jobs and their work at home, which is uppermost, free choice or constraint? Do women devote time to home and family because they specifically prefer to or because they do not seriously conceive of any alternative? Realistically, what alternatives do exist? What models can be found of a different division of labor, where women are not expected to specialize in child care and where "home responsibilities" are not automatically assigned to women?

To design and construct such models will provide new alternatives for the future status of women—and for men. If women's "home responsibilities" represent an assignment and a lack of choice, this is equally true of the responsibilities assigned to men. If the woman is the homemaker, the man is the bread-winner. The assumption that men will provide financial support is also taken for granted. That home and family depend, economically, upon husband and father is a precept lying so deep within the male psyche that long periods of unemployment when he cannot fulfill these obligations cause severe emotional stress. To have women dependent has become so ingrained, for a man, that the employment in his own organization of a bright, capable woman can still appear as a threat to his masculinity. The next revolution can widen the choices for men and for women, and can offer young men realistic alternatives to the uninter-rupted work history—the forty-five years' work experience—that now differenti-ates them from women. Twenty-one years after Alva Myrdal published her book, *Women's Two Roles*, still describes the situation for women because the first revolution has merely expanded the number of women with two roles—market employment and work at home. The second revolution must deal with the work at home so that it is no longer assigned on the basis of sex and so that we no longer think of *women* with role conflicts.

Reorganizing an existing operation or changing a given activity requires, first, an objective analysis of what is going on. Realistically, of what do these "home responsibilities" consist, and what does the occupation of homemaker entail?

Work at home contains two kinds of productive services: caring for persons and caring for the dwelling place and its furnishings. From the viewpoint of the economics of human capital, both services appear as maintenance, akin to the regular lubrication and overhaul of machinery, the painting and polishing of buildings, and the replenishment of inventory in a factory. As capital, human beings yield a return over time—by working productively or performing useful functions. Consequently, keeping human beings fed, warm, clothed, clean, and even happy keeps them productive and efficient. Therefore, a considerable part of household tasks can be subsumed under the term, *consumer maintenance.*

For adults, "consumer maintenance" is clearly an individual responsibility and can be supplied in many ways. One can rent a room and eat in the local delicatessen or live in a hotel with valet and cleaning services and make the rounds of restaurants. One can travel and enjoy a variety of living arrangements purchased on land, sea, and in the air. One can hire other people to prepare food and do cleaning; the hiring arrangements can be casual or long term. One can live alone and provide varying proportions of "consumer maintenance" to oneself, or one can live with other people and share these functions.

There are two reasons to use the term, *consumer maintenance*, which was invented several years ago.[14] One is to emphasize the economic nature of these activities, which have never found their way into the Gross National Product. (It is erroneous to assume, as some have, that economists are either stupid or sexist in omitting the value of homework from this calculation. Many other unpaid activities, including work done by men, have not yet been calculated in the GNP.) The term, *consumer maintenance*, clearly identifies these home activities of feeding, cleaning, and caring as productive, and in no sense peripheral, luxurious, or exploitative. The second reason to use this term is to emphasize that a large part of the so-called "home responsibilities" of women actually consists of household and personal responsibilities of individual human beings.

Men who are not married take care of themselves, some of them quite well indeed. The division of labor assumed does not conform to the reality where single men own homes, cook, do housecleaning, and have a stock of clean shirts and socks without holes. Nor does it encompass the reality of adults devising living arrangements in various successful combinations, from two college roommates later sharing an apartment to the two friendly couples who build a vacation home together. Consequently, the time is long overdue for some rethinking of the term, *home responsibilities,* as a variable in a regression analysis of women's employment, or the term, *household occupation*, used as a classification for women, but not for men. The care and feeding of adult persons goes on wherever adult persons live. The functions of housekeeping, doing the wash, shopping, paying bills, getting meals, giving parties, and cleaning up after them occur in every adult person's life. These activities have not been developed by women specializing in women's work at home. "Consumer maintenance" for adults may be a large part of the productive services performed by housewives, but "consumer maintenance" would still exist if there were no housewives.

A different situation exists with children and adults who, because of their age or disability, cannot care for themselves adequately. Probably the term, *consumer maintenance*, is inappropriate here, since these people do not produce anything and do not, therefore, resemble machinery to be kept oiled or rollingstock to be kept fueled. The economic aspect of caring for old people or for those who are disabled differs from the economics of caring for children—society arranges to "insure against" the misfortunes of old age or disability, but to "invest in the future of" the youngsters. Finally, the nonmarket character of child care looms large: most children have a direct relation to the adults who care for them, that is, they are offspring and parents, they make up the social unit known as the family.

It seems to be well established that child care, from birth through some indeterminate age, requires more personal involvement than does adult care.[15] The facilities of hotels, airplanes, hired services, or cafeterias may yield "consumer maintenance" for adults but would not suffice for the healthy growth and development of a child. Children need nurturing, which is a kind of care that cannot be provided by children for themselves and is not always available in the market. The most common model of such care has been the mother who nurtures her child, although the function of child-rearing exists separately from childbearing in many different cultural settings. Even this society contains single parents who are men. However, the mother has generally been assigned the function of child-rearing and, generally, it means that she stays at home. It is, in fact, this locational requirement that has led to women's specializing in household tasks. In effect, she may as well be useful while she's home and so she spends the rest of her time in caring for adults. The occupation of homemaker has grown out of the occupation of child-rearer.

Viewed in this way, none of the so-called "home responsibilities" of women are intrinsically feminine. The occupation of child-rearer need not be filled only by a mother. Consequently, the second revolution faces no insurmountable technical obstacles to a different division of labor. There is already scope for considerable realignment of tasks. Existing technology and institutional arrangements can shift more consumer maintenance outside the home. Young people can be educated and socialized to share more fully the tasks of "consumer maintenance" with the other people with whom they live. We can urge more emphasis on parenting and less on mothering, more paternal leave with newborn babies, and more fathers to take custody of their children when parents split up. However, massive change will require more than education, consciousness-raising, or social enlightenment, which are all basically "soft" programs. A revolution means positive and drastic action—specific measures to shift employment within the home.

At this point we will propose several alternatives for social change, all of which would lead to a different status for women and for men. I believe these proposals emphasize our common humanity and would enhance our potential for individual development and for personal change in the direction of self-realization. They would certainly also alter the structure of society.

First, let us specify the division of labor entailed with marriage and a family. As no-fault divorce is extended, a compulsory marriage contract should be introduced, as equally important. If marriage continues to be a legal state, one for which licenses must be obtained, then the law offers an opportunity for protecting, not the marriage itself, but the individual growth and enhancement of each partner. Marriage holds dangers that require considered thought, not just a waiting period before being granted a license. Guarding against the threat of disabling infection by a spouse requires more than freedom from venereal disease. A marriage contract would have two people work out their own division of labor on the basis of their own rational decisions rather than by relying on assumptions that later prove controversial. The state's standard marriage contract would embody specific agreement about financial arrangements, household arrangements, and provisions for child care, and could be amplified by mutual consent. Such a contract, signed in order to obtain a marriage license, could serve as a basis for later civil suit with or without divorce. However, that is not the intention. Primarily, the contract would delineate the separation, analyzed above, between the institution of marriage and the existence of home responsibilities.

Next, compulsory child-care insurance to which both parents would contribute equally. Divorce insurance has already been suggested as logical, in view of the rising divorce rate, but except for the costs of a brief transition period or of divorce proceedings (which should diminish as no-fault laws spread) little economic risk is present for adults in a marriage dissolution. Such an economic risk does exist for dependent children. If the offspring—not the mother—have the protection of insurance, then caring for the children of divorced parents can become an economically viable occupation, perhaps for one or the other parent, but perhaps for someone else entirely. That the biological parents of a child may be totally unfitted, or not best fitted, to nurture the child has been recognized in various court proceedings. A seminal book, *Beyond the Best Interests of the Child*, argues that much wider acceptance of this notion is long overdue.[16] The psychological or emotional parent of the child needs recognition and support from state and society. It should be added that the best interests of adult women are not served by the existing assumption on the part of many courts that young children belong with their mother. Child-care insurance provides a way for the continued growth and development of a woman as an individual person, despite the fact that she has given birth.[17] Requiring compulsory child-care insurance would specifically separate the functions of childbearing from child-rearing.

It would, furthermore, emphasize that marriage and a family represent a way of spending income, a set of consumption choices like buying a stereo set, a trip to Europe, or a college education. Like other consumption goods, marriage and the family come in several models, and we would urge measures to favor those models where the woman is not, automatically, the homemaker. The most powerful means of accomplishing this would do away with the economic status of dependent spouse, which nearly always means dependent wife or widow. We would repeal provisions for a dependent spouse in determining taxes, social security benefits, wage levels, fringe benefits, or any other form of earned income. While the result would be a radical alteration in the framework of decision making, there are sound economic arguments for this change.[18]

It rests first on the recognition that earnings from work—and most income in this country is paid for working—is inherently a personal, individual activity. The language recognizes the direct link between job and person. *I* teach, *he* dances, *she* operates, *he* is a jeweler, and *she* is a lawyer. The earnings from work therefore represent a payment to the individual. How that individual spends the earnings, and in particular if the payment gets used for other people, cannot change the relationship between individual worker and individual job. What this means, quite simply, is that the minimum wage cannot be calculated in terms of what it costs to support a family. Nor can *any* wage *or* salary *or* fringe benefit be so justified. One is paid *for* working, *for* accomplishing a task, or *for* carrying out duties, not *because* one has children, an aged father, or a disabled sister. It means that social security benefits should not be higher for a retired worker with a dependent wife than for a retired single worker. Wives work all of their lives; let them be entitled to social security benefits in their own right, not as someone's dependent.[19] It means that tax rates should be equal for all persons with the same income. Being head of household, married and filing a joint return or single status should not affect the individual as taxpayer.[20] By removing the complexities of tax advantages or benefit loss, the decision to marry can become, as it should be, a matter of human relationship and individual choice. By letting wages and salaries revert to their proper *economic* functions of paying for individual work, the question of supporting people and perhaps of providing adequate income can become, as it should be, a matter of human responsbility and willingness to care for others.

So far the proposals outlined would make the role of dependent homemaker more costly and, that alone, would encourage a different division of labor between the sexes. It would probably also result in substantial institutional changes, with recognized money wages being paid to homemakers of whatever sex or marital status, for example. However, two other proposals would make employment at home more attractive to men. The first concerns the growing number of families with no husband or father present.

There seems little reason, under existing circumstances, to expect any change in the trend exhibited over the past decade showing a rapid and significant rise in the number of families consisting of mother and children alone.[21] Such families constitute the largest welfare burden today, and income payments for these mothers and children are minimal. One illustrative figure will serve, perhaps, from the population survey of 1973. In that year there were about 27 million families with both parents and at least one child: over half of them had incomes over $12,000 and fewer than one in five received less than $6,000. By contrast, over half the families containing no husband or father received incomes of less than $6,000 and about one in five of these mothers with children received less than $3,000. Families dependent on a single woman number five million; they contain ten million children. These children are not responsible for their poverty. The difference between their lot and that of the 55 million children in the other families stems from the simple fact that their mothers got pregnant but they have no fathers. The welfare system that supports them is called "Aid to Families of Dependent Children," but in fact payments are made, grudgingly in these hard times, because the children and their mothers are dependent.

One response to this situation has been to urge measures strengthening the family as an institution; another has been to intensify a search for absent fathers. Representative Martha Griffith's superb studies of income and welfare exemplify the first approach, but the bill she introduced into the last Congress has received no serious attention.[22] The second approach means that the Department of Health, Education and Welfare will now assist any woman, not just those on welfare, in her search for the man who is delinquent in child support payments. However, the following suggestion would improve the economic status of all mothers and of all women while providing special help for the ten million children on welfare.

On the grounds that male responsibility for these children has been success-fully shifted, I propose a special tax to pay for the total welfare benefits of families headed by women, and sufficient to increase these benefits so as to wipe out the income differential between poor children with only a mother and well-off children with two parents. The tax would be levied on all men. It would be a flat "head tax," shared equally among all men. Two kinds of exemptions would be allowed: first for men with medical evidence of sterility, and second for men engaged in home responsibilities or in caring for children at home. The tax would represent, in economists' terms, a massive shift of income from men who are capable of impregnating women, to women who have been impregnated and left alone to care for the results.[a] While its immediate impact would be to improve the status of poor children, it would also reduce the crushing burden of "home responsibilities" for their mothers by enabling more consumer mainte-nance services to be purchased. One likely result, of course, would be that more welfare mothers would seek market employment.

However, work at home will still be attractive to many married women

[a]The tax would not be discriminatory because it could be levied on putative sperm donors, a category referring to physical ability and not sex, per se. I have used the term "men" in the text as a shorthand reference to putative sperm donors.

because of the low level of wages they can expect to earn outside the home. The remedy lies not in raising the minimum wage so that "women's jobs" will pay more, nor in legislating affirmative action programs, but in making home employment more attractive to men, in comparison to their alternative earnings from outside employment. One way to do this also relies on taxes.

A tax can be used most effectively to direct productive activity. Thus, if we tax automobiles on the basis of their gasoline consumption workers will be shifted from making "gas-guzzlers" to making more economical cars—or even more bicycles. If we tax the earnings of salesworkers more than the salaries of janitors then people will shift from selling to cleaning. If, therefore, we tax the earnings of men more heavily than those of women, we will increase the *relative* attractiveness of work at home for men, and the *relative* attractiveness of work outside the home for women. There are two ways of doing this: either by taxing the employer when jobs are more heavily filled by men than by women,[b] or by taxing the male earner more than the female earner with the same level of income. Each would have different effects on prices and markets, but either would make men consider, more seriously, employment at home as an alternative occupation.

The list of positive programs can, of course, be amplified. We suspect the immediate usefulness of all such suggestions lies in arousing an audience reaction. Merely jolting people from their accustomed ways of thinking can be a step toward achieving a favorable climate for social change. These suggestions, both separately and taken as a package, would hasten the second revolution, where a new division of labor does away with the notion of the home responsibilities of women. However, they also envision women as independent people, responsible to themselves as individuals and to others as contributing members of society. We hope that whatever alternative social actions we choose, we make certain they have this impact, so that the future status of women becomes irrelevant, and we share a mutual concern for the status of human beings.

Notes

1. Alice Rivlin, *Systematic Thinking for Social Action* (Washington, D.C.: Brookings Institution, 1971).

2. Evelyne Sullerot, *Woman, Society, and Change* (London: Weidenfeld and Nicolson, 1971); Margaret Mead, *Male and Female* (New York: Morrow, 1949).

3. Donald Cymrat and Lucy B. Mallan, "Wife's Earnings as a Source of Family Income," U.S. Department of Health, Education and Welfare, Social Security Administration, Office of Research Statistics, Note No. 10, 1974, April 30, 1974; Carolyn Shaw Bell, "Working Women's Contributions to Family Income," *Eastern Economic Journal*, 1, no. 3 (July 1974).

[b]The British experience with the selective employment tax is of interest here.

4. See, for example, Martha O. Blaxall and Barbara Reagan, eds., *Occupational Segregation: Past, Present, and Future* (Chicago: University of Chicago Press, 1975).

5. B.R. Bergmann and I. Adelman, "The Economic Role of Women," *American Economic Review* 63, no. 4 (September 1973); Di Cesare and Constance Begh, "Change In the Occupational Structure of U.S. Jobs," *Monthly Labor Review* 98, no. 3 (March 1975).

6. Michael Young and Peter Willmott, *The Symmetrical Family* (New York: Random House, 1973).

7. Gary Becker, *The Economics of Discrimination* (Chicago: University of Chicago Press, 1957); K.J. Arrow, "The Theory of Discrimination," in Orley Ashenfelter and Albert Rees, eds., *Discrimination in Labor Markets* (Princeton: Princeton University Press, 1973); Barbara Bergmann, "The Effect on White Incomes of Discrimination in Employment," *Journal of Political Economy* (March/April, 1971); "Occupational Segregation, Wages, and Profits," *Eastern Economic Journal* 1, no. 2 (April 1974).

8. Isobel Sawhille, "The Earnings Gap: Research Needs and Issues," unpublished paper, 1974.

9. William G. Bowen and T. Aldrich Finigan, *The Economics of Labor Force Participation* (Princeton: Princeton University Press, 1969); James Sweet, *Women in the Labor Forces* (New York: Seminar Press, 1973).

10. *Economic Report of the President, 1973, 1974, 1975* (Washington, D.C.: U.S. Government Printing Office).

11. Gary Becker, "A Theory of the Allocation of Time," *Economic Journal* 75, no. 3 (September 1965).

12. Carolyn Shaw Bell, "Economics, Sex, and Gender," *Social Science Quarterly* 55, no. 3 (December 1974).

13. Ibid.

14. Carolyn Shaw Bell, "Full Employment Implications for Women," *Social Policy* 3, no. 3 (September/October, 1972) and in *Public Service Employment* (New York: Praeger, 1973).

15. Jessie Bernard, *The Future of Motherhood* (New York: Dial Press, 1974).

16. Joseph Goldstein, Anna Freud, and Albert J. Solnit, *Beyond the Best Interests of the Child* (Riverside, N.J.: Free Press, 1973).

17. Angela Barron McBride, *The Growth and Development of Mothers* (New York: Harper & Row, 1973).

18. Carolyn Shaw Bell, "Should Every Job Support A Family?" *The Public Interest* no. 40 (Summer 1975).

19. "The Treatment of Women Under Social Security and Private Pension Plans," *Economic Problems of Women*, Hearings before the Joint Economic Committee, Congress of the United States, 93rd Congress, 1st Session, July 25, 1973.

20. Georgia Dullea, "Marriage Tax," *New York Times*, March 27, 1975, p. 26.

21. U.S. Bureau of the Census, *Current Population Reports*, "Money Income

in 1973 of Families and Persons in the United States," Series P-60, No. 97, issued January 1975; "Characteristics of the Low-Income Population: 1973," Series P-60, No. 98, issued January 1975; "Household and Family Characteristics: March 1974" Series P-20, No. 276, issued February 1975.

22. "Income Security for Americans: Recommendations of the Public Welfare Study," Report of the Subcommittee on Fiscal Policy of the Joint Economic Committee, Congress of the United States (Washington, D.C.: U.S. Governemnt Printing Office, December 5, 1974).

Index

Index

abortion, 32-33
Abramson, P., 82n
Academia, women in, xvi, 15-23
academic appointments, 18-21
achievement motivation, 4-7
Adams, M., 99n, 100n, 109n
Adelman, I., 125n
Affirmative Action, 4
age: of female black legislators, 88; of
  single women, 36; of women in U.S.,
  37-38
Almond, G., 97n
ambition, in politics, 91, 94
antinatalism, 68, 77
Arber, S., 62n
Arrow, K.J., 125
Astin, H.S., 19
athletics, women in, 117-118
attitudes, toward working women,
  60-62
Avery, W., 84n

Baerwaldt, N., 60n
Baker, E.F., 25n
Bancroft, G., 25n
Bayer, A.E., 19
Becker, G., 125, 127n
Bell, C.S., 124n, 127n, 129n, 133n
Berelson, B., 68n
Berent, J., 33n
Bergman, E., 67n
Bergmann, B.R., 125
Berkov, B., 33n
Bernard, J., 15, 130n
Billingsley, A., 94n
birth: cohorts, 26-29; rates, 29-38,
  67-68, 72-74
blacks: achievement, 3-4; birth rates,
  34-36; education, 3-4; employment,
  45, 54-60; income, 49; political effi-
  cacy, 83, 93-94; political protest, 84,
  111; views of liberation, 90-91;
  volunteer political activities, 84,
  111; voters in presidential elections,
  108, 109, 111; voters in South, 103;
  women state legislators, xviii, 81-96
Blake, J., 32n, 68, 70n
Blaxall, M.O., 124n

Bowen, W.G., 25n, 44n, 45n, 125n
Brazer, H.E., 60n
Bumpass, L.L., 29n, 32n, 34, 60-62
Burnham, W.D., 100n

Cain, G., 45n
Carey, A., Jr., 84n
Carnegie Commission, 4
Carter, H., 37n
Cartter, A., 19
Centra, J., 21
Chafe, W.H., 100n, 102, 106, 110
Chasteen, E., 68n
Chesler, P., 70n
childbearing: ages of and labor force
  participation, 26-29; expectations,
  18
child care, 69-70, 130-134
Clark, R., 83
Clayton, E.T., 83
Cohen, W.J., 60n
Colby, Bainbridge, 102
Committee on Woman Suffrage, U.S.
  Senate (1913), 101n
Conlin, R.B., 116n, 117n, 118n, 119n,
  120n
consumer maintenance, 129-130
contraception, 31-38, 67-68, 69-73, 77
Crummine, J., 6n
Cymrat, D., 124n
Czajka, J., 62

David, M.H., 60n
Davis, K., 68
Democrats, 92, 106, 110
demography: impact of on labor force,
  25-66; impact of on status of
  women, 67
Di Cesare, C.B., 50, 124n
divorce, 29, 74, 131
Dixon, R.B., 69n
domicile, 118-119
Dullea, G., 132n
Durand, J.D., 25n

Earnings. See Income
Easterlin, R.A., 25n, 34n
Economic Problems of Women, 132n

Economic Report of the President,
1973, 1974, 1975, 126n
economy: analysis of women's status,
125-127; anthropological theory,
70-71; effects of on academic market, 16-18, 20-21; effects of on fertility rates, 34, 69; effects of on
women's political roles, 111-112
education: of black state legislators,
85-87; impact of on employment,
44-47, 58-59, 74-76; impact of on
fertility, 69-74; impact of on income, 49, 52; impact of on politics,
83; legal status of women, 115,
116-118; political offices of, 83;
rates of for women, 37, 39; women
in higher education, xvi, xviii, 10-12,
15-24
employment: of black state legislators,
86-87; effects of mothers' on children, 62; expectations of women,
17-18, 127-128; and fertility, 69-73;
historical patterns of women, 25-66;
impact on by education, 44-47; occupations of women, 47-49; 50-51,
57-59, 75-76, 124-128; proportion
of females in 1920, 72-73; sex differentials, 44-49; trends of women,
25-66, 124-125
enrollment trends, xviii, 16, 21-22
Epstein, S., 9n
Equal Employment Opportunity Act.
See Title VII
Equal Employment Opportunity Commission, 43, 115-116
Equal Pay Act, xv, xviii, 76, 115
Equal Rights Amendment, 67, 71,
76-77, 102, 121, 123
Etaugh, C., 62n
Executive Order 11246 (as amended),
xv, 76

family size, 31-38, 68, 88-89
Federal jobs, women in, 97
"feme sole trader," 119
Fenz, W., 9n
Ferriss, A.L., 25n, 37n
fertility: control, 68; and female em-
ployment, 68-78; and female status,
67-80; rates of, xviii, 29-38, 68
Finigan, T.A., 25n, 44n, 45n, 125n
Flaim, P.D., 74n

Fracy, D.P., 99-100
Franklin, J.H., 83n
Freud, A., 131n
Furniss, W.T., 17n
future status of women, 123-136

Gardner, J., 22
geography, of female black state legis-
lators, 85-86
Glick, P.C., 37n
goals of women, 1-14, 18
Goldstein, J., 131n
Gosnell, H.F., 103, 104
Graham, P.A., 17n
Grant, D.R., 90n
Grant, W.V., 37n
Gray, V., 67n
Gruberg, M., 89n
Gutwillig, J.G., 43n

Hardin, G., 68n
Harrison, E.C., 84n
Hayghe, H., 74n
Higher Education Act of 1972 (Title
IX), 76, 117-118
Hill, F., 84n
Hill, R., 94n
Hinde, R.A., 9
Hoffman, L.W., 62n
Horner, M., 4-6
Hyman, H.H., 82

Illiterates, females in 1920, 72-73
income: of families, 133; as payments
to individuals, 132-133; of professional women, xvii; sex differences
in, xvi, xvii, 19-20, 116, 125-127; of
women, 49-59
incumbency of female black state
legislators, 89-90, 92

Jennings, M.K., 82n
Jensen, R.J., 100n
Jones, E.F., 33n
Jones, J.H., 81n

Kagan, J., 9
Keller, S., 70n
Key, V.O., 85, 103
King, Mae C., 81n
Kleppner, P.J., 100n
Kohn, M., 9-10

Koontz, E.D., 43n
Krause, W.R., 97

Labor force. *See* Employment
Langton, K.P., 82n
Lansing, M., 83, 107, 108
Laurence, J., 82n
League of Women Voters, 110
Lester, R.A., 4
Levine, Adeline, 6n
Lind, C.G., 37n
Lipman-Blumen, J., 2
Long, C., 25n
Lowe, V., 43n, 47n
Lyons, S., 82n

McBride, A.B., 131n
McEaddy, B.J., 75n
McIntosh, S., 70n
McPhee, W.A., 103
Mallan, L.B., 124n
marriage: contracts, 131-133; division
    of labor, 131-133; of female black
    state legislators, 88; labor force pat-
    terns of married women, 29-44,
    74-76; legal status of women,
    118-121
Marvick, D., 82n
Mason, K.O., 60, 61n, 62
matriarch, black women seen as, 81-82
Matthews, D.R., 83, 84n
Mead, M., 124n
Merriam, C.E., 104
Merton, R., 3
Milbrath, L., 97n
Mill, J.S., 4, 98
Miller, Neal, 8
mobilization of voters, 104-106
Moltz, H., 9
Moore, W., 23
Morgan, J., 60
Murphy, I.L., 97

National Center for Health Statistics,
    29n, 30n, 37n
National Fertility Study, 1970, 60
National Organization for Women, 77,
    110
National Women Suffrage Association,
    100
New Deal era, effects on women, 106,
    107

Nie, N.H., 97n
Nixon, H.D., 90n
Norton, A., 37n
Nye, F.I., 62n

Oakley, Ann, 10
occupation. *See* Employment
Oppenheimer, V., 17n, 25n, 75n
Orbell, J., 84n

Parke, R., Jr., 33n
Parnes, H., 17-18
part-time faculty arrangements, 20
personality, 7-10
Pierce, J., 84n
Pitkin, H., 93n
Pohlman, E., 70n
political efficacy: of black women, 82,
    93-94, 111; of women, 98, 102-106,
    109-112
political participants, history of
    women as, 97-114
political party affiliation of black
    women state legislators. *See* Demo-
    crats.
political protest of blacks, 84, 111
politics: of black women, 81-96; his-
    tory of women in, 97-114; women in
    state legislatures, xix, 7, 10, 97
population policy, 67-80
pronatalism, 67-68, 77
property rights of women, 118
"protective" laws, 115
Prothro, J.W., 83, 84n

Reagan, B., 124n
Reed, J.S., 82
Reed, R.H., 70n
Reid, I., 84
*Report of the Subcommittee on Fiscal
    Policy of the Joint Economic Com-
    mittee*, 133n
reproductive decisions, 67-70
Ridley, J.C., 70n
Rich, W., 69n
Rindfuss, R.R., 33n
Rivlin, A., 123n
roles: in education, 116-118; flexi-
    bility in politics, 94; political roles,
    97-114; role incompatibility, 69-70;
    sex roles, 60-62, 116-118, 123, 128
Rossi, A., 17, 22

Ruhter, W.E., 19n
Rusk, J.G., 98n, 103n, 109n
Ryder, N.B., 29n, 31

Sanday, P.R., 70-71
Sawhille, I., 125n
Schlesinger, J., 90, 94n
Schooler, C., 10
Schultz, T.P., 69n, 73n
Scott, E., 19
Scott, R., 112n
seniority, 16
Seymour, C., 99-100
Sirageldin, I., 60n
Sklar, J., 33n
Smith, R.A., 103n
Smuts, R.W., 25-26
socialization, 4-7, 61, 68, 130; of
  black women to politics, 81; of
  women to politics, 102-106
Solnit, A.J., 131n
Spokeswoman, 68n
Staples, R., 82n, 94n
state legislatures, xix, 7, 10, 81-96, 97
Stiehm, J., 112n
Stimson, C., 77n
Stucker, J.J., 82, 98n, 100n, 102n,
  103n, 109n
success, fear of, 4-7
suffrage: adoption before 1920,
  101-102; effects of on birth rates,
  71-73; history of, 97-114; school
  elections, 99-100, 103; of widows,
  99
Sullerot, E., 124n
Survey Research Center, 106
Sweet, J.A., 27, 29n, 35, 36n, 43n,
  45n, 47, 51n, 57n, 125n

Taeuber, I.B. and Taeuber, C., 25n
taxation: equality of, 132; legal effects
  on women, 120; proposals, 133-134
tenure, 16, 19

Tingsten, H., 102, 106
Title VII, 1964 Civil Rights Act, xv,
  43, 76, 115

Udry, J.R., 69n
United States Bureau of the Census,
  xvi, xvii, xviii, 27n, 32n, 36, 37n,
  38, 39, 52, 54, 59, 86, 107, 109,
  132n
United States Bureau of Labor Statistics, 27, 28, 40n, 41, 42n, 47, 48,
  52, 53, 55, 56, 58
United States Commission on Population Growth and the American
  Future, 70, 77
universities, women in, xviii, 4, 15-24

values, 1-14
Verba, S., 97n
volunteer political activities: of black
  women, 84, 111; of women,
  110-112
voters, women as, 97-114
Voting Rights Act, 1965, 83, 108
voting turnout, 100, 102-109

Waldman, E., 74n, 75n
Weller, R.W., 69
Werner, E.E., 86n
Westoff, C.F., 29n, 31, 33n
Westoff, L.A., 29n
Willingham, A.W., 81n
Willmott, P., 125n
Women's Equity Education Act of
  1974, 76
Women's Political Caucus, 97
women's political status, history of,
  97-114

Young, A.M., 74n
Young, M., 125n

About the Contributors

Carolyn Shaw Bell is Katherine Coman Professor of Economics at Wellesley College. In addition to her academic activities, Professor Bell is currently a member of the Advisory Committee on Women to the Secretary of Labor; the American Economic Association Executive Committee; Board of Directors, Association for Evolutionary Economics; Board of Overseers, Amos Tuck Graduate School of Business Administration at Dartmouth College; and the Federal Advisory Council on Unemployment Insurance. Her professional credits include publication of five books and numerous articles.

Roxanne Barton Conlin earned her law degree from Drake University in 1966. She is Assistant Attorney General for the State of Iowa, where she is Director of the Iowa Civil Rights Section, Department of Justice. She is State Chairperson of the Iowa Women's Political Caucus and a member of the Iowa Commission on the Status of Women. She was chosen by *Redbook* Magazine as one of "44 Women Who Could Save America," and received the award for outstanding service of civil liberties, presented by the Iowa Civil Liberties Union in 1974.

Cynthia Fuchs Epstein is Professor of Sociology, Queens College of the City University of New York. In addition to teaching, Professor Epstein is senior research associate at the Bureau of Applied Social Research at Columbia University. She has worked as a consultant for the Advisory Commission on the Economic Role of Women for the White House; American Telephone and Telegraph Company; the White House Conference on Children; and the Commission on Population Growth and the American Future. She is the author of four books and numerous articles on the roles of women in society.

Virginia Gray is Assistant Professor of Political Science at the University of Minnesota, Minneapolis. Prior to teaching at Minnesota, Professor Gray taught at Washington University in St. Louis and the University of Kentucky. She is the author of publications in the field of public policy in the United States and is co-editor of a volume on the political issues in U.S. population policy. She has presented papers at a number of professional meetings; currently she is chairwoman of the Midwest Political Science Association Committee on the Status of Women.

Juanita M. Kreps is Vice President and James B. Duke Professor of Economics, Duke University. Prior to her appointment as Vice President of Duke University, Professor Kreps was Dean of the Women's College. In addition to leading textbooks in economics, she has written extensively in the areas of labor and manpower, and in the economics of aging. At present, Professor Kreps is President-elect of the Southern Economics Association and serves on the Board of Directors of the J.C. Penney Company, the New York Stock Exchange, and Western Electric. She holds a Presidential appointment to the National Manpower Commission.

Jewel Prestage is a Professor of Political Science and Chairwoman of the Department at Southern University. Her career has had many distinctions. She was the first black woman to receive a Ph.D. in political science in the United States. She was the youngest recipient of a Ph.D. from the University of Iowa and she was the first woman and first black to serve as President of the Southwestern Social Science Association. In 1974 she was honored as the outstanding faculty member at Southern University.

John J. Stucker is an Assistant Professor of Political Science and Director of the Social and Behavioral Sciences Laboratory at the University of South Carolina. Professor Stucker has been a guest scholar at the Brookings Institution and is the author of several publications dealing with historical patterns of political participation. His doctoral dissertation from the University of Michigan dealt with the impact of woman suffrage on voter participation in the United States.

James A. Sweet is an Associate Professor of Sociology and Director of the Center for Demography and Ecology at the University of Wisconsin, Madison. The study of women's involvement in the labor force has occupied most of his academic career. He is the author of numerous papers and articles, most of which analyze various aspects of the relationship of female fertility and employment. In addition, he is the author of a textbook on women in the U.S. labor force. Along with being the Director of the Center for Demography and Ecology, he is associated with the Institute for Research on Poverty.

About the Editor

Laurily Keir Epstein is Assistant to the Chancellor at Washington University in St. Louis. She also teaches at Washington University and for the Central Michigan University Graduate Program in Public Administration. She received the Ph.D. in Political Science from Washington University in 1974; her major fields of interest are American political behavior, public opinion, and electoral history. Dr. Epstein is a member of the American Academy for the Advancement of Science, the American Political Science Association (member of the Committee on Pre-Collegiate Education), the Midwest Political Science Association, and the Missouri Political Science Association.